celebrate
life

celebrate

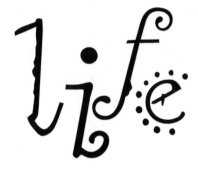

Rituals for Home and Church

Peter Young

United Church Press
Cleveland, Ohio

United Church Press, Cleveland, Ohio 44115
© 1999 by Peter Young

Library of Congress Cataloging-in-Publication Data
Young, Peter, 1930 Apr. 9–
    Celebrate life : rituals for home and church / Peter Young.
        p.   cm.
    Includes bibliographical references.
    ISBN 0-8298-1294-6 (pbk. : alk. paper)
    1. Rites and ceremonies.   2. Life change events—Religious aspects—
    Christianity.   I. Title.
    BV176.Y68 1999
    264—dc21   98-50332
                                                                            CIP

Contents

Preface

•••••••••••

There is an unease, even a dis-ease, permeating our land. When asked to describe the unease, we hear many answers: loss of self-worth, violence and abuse, alcoholism, drug abuse, disappearance of family values, loss of moral restraints and guidelines, sexual promiscuity, crime, homelessness, joblessness, racism, poverty—social problems that appear overwhelming and insoluble.

In response, politicians offer solutions. Sociologists offer solutions. Economists offer solutions. Think tanks offer solutions. Members of the clergy offer solutions. Psychiatrists offer solutions. Counselors offer solutions. Educators offer solutions. Physical fitness experts offer solutions. Nonetheless, the unease, the dis-ease continues.

Some astute observers of the scene, however, are beginning to point out that one of the most significant trends in our society has been the loss of unifying rituals. While this has been taking place, there has also been a quantum leap in individualism and in loss of community.

Tom F. Driver, in *The Magic of Ritual*, says that this is an age in which the decline of ritual sensibility—particularly in the Western industrialized nations—has become a threat to the survival of life on earth.[1]

Several years ago, *Habits of the Heart*[2] described one of today's major moral dilemmas as the conflict between our rugged individualism and our real need for community. Our religious life reflects this dilemma.

There is such an emphasis on religious experience as personal and individual that we have lost the sense of corporateness, the sense of belonging to a larger community of faith, in which the religious experience really has meaning. At the same time, the church too often has been more interested in maintaining its own institutional life than in supporting and strengthening the lives of its members. As a result, there is a wide gap between the home and the church, a gap that actually contributes to the general unease, the general dis-ease in the land.

Margaret Mead once asked: "How can we give people rituals that will carry them through crises, rituals that will enable each individual, however deep his grief or confusion, however high his excitement, to reach out to the feelings of others who have experienced the same thing and to his own previous experiences, and to reach out in such a way that gives depth and meaning to the present?"[3]

We human beings have always developed familiar patterns of behavior around various life-cycle situations, the milestones and times of transitions in our lives—for example, birthday celebrations. In addition, we have developed these familiar patterns in connection with the cycle of the calendar year—for example, thanksgiving/harvest festivals. We also have developed these patterns in our corporate religious life. These patterns of behavior we call rituals, rites, ceremonies, celebrations.

The primary reason we do this is because these patterns provide a means of integrating the individual into a particular segment of society; they aid in the transition from one phase of life to another. These patterns are particularly important in the formation of spiritual values and in the transmission of the faith from one generation to another. They provide a significant teaching/learning atmosphere while providing children with a sense of safety and security.

In addition, these religious rituals provide the individual as well as the community of faith with stability and power in the face of stress and in times of significant change or loss. Religious rituals are unifying, ordering, stabilizing, maintaining , transforming, and liberating (or at least they should be!).

Celebrate Life attempts to answer Margaret Mead's question. It has been created to provide a means of developing familiar patterns of behavior that help bridge the gap between home and church, in the sincere hope of providing depth and meaning to our lives.

The introduction to *Celebrate Life* shows why rituals play such an important role in our lives and why the loss of same has contributed to the dis-ease in the land.

"Celebratory Rituals for the Home" attempts to provide the home with ways to celebrate the milestones, the times of joy, the times of transition, and the times of trauma in the life of each member of the family, as well as to provide celebrations of preparation for the larger community of faith gatherings.

It is hoped that these rituals will aid families in the transmission of their faith from one generation to another and will help in times of stress.

"Celebratory Rituals for the Church" attempts to provide the church with ways to recognize the milestones—the times of joy, the times of transition, and the times of trauma—in the lives of its members, as well as to offer some additional celebrations for the gathered community of faith.

One word of caution: The suggested rituals and celebrations are only designed to serve as patterns or samples, to serve as guides for the development of your own rituals and celebrations. "Flexibility" and "freedom" are key words.

May *Celebrate Life* be a means of deepening the sense of God's empowering presence in your midst and of strengthening the relationship between your family and the larger family of your community of faith.

Acknowledgments

· ·

My deepest appreciation goes to the members of the Mayville Congregational United Church of Christ, Mayville, North Dakota, for providing me with the opportunity to draw together all of the components of *Celebrate Life*, through sabbatical studies, through participating in and responding to many of the celebratory rituals contained in this work, and through the encouragement the members and friends of the church have given me. In addition, I would like to express my love and heartfelt thanks to my wife, Anne, for her encouragement, even prodding, throughout the entire process of writing *Celebrate Life*, for her proofreading, and for her constructive criticism. And, finally to all of my colleagues in ministry who expressed a desire for the material here provided, thank you for your support.

Introduction: $\mathcal{S}$aying Yes to Life

∙∙

"if it be granted
that we say yea
to a single moment, then
in so doing we have said yea
not only to ourselves,
but to all existence."

To celebrate is to explain who we are and to say yea ceremonially.
What happens to the man
happens to the whole human rule.
A man reacts and responds to what is other than himself
and he reacts and responds to the many that he is inside himself.
He creates many small ceremonies and celebrations all day long—
if he has any health.
He laughs and cries and shouts
in expressing the delight and sorrow and anger
which arise in him—or descend into him.
These ceremonies underline the importance of each emotion and
the emotions are what keep the human race running.

When he refuses to form outside of him what starts to grow
from within reacting to what is out, he stunts and paralyzes
and warps the stuff that makes him
and becomes deformed
strikes out destructively
becomes inept—not able to become human.
He stops being—at least in part.

—*Corita Kent*[1]

Rituals Help Us Say Yes to Life's Experiences

What Corita Kent is saying so beautifully in her poem is that when we are truly alive as persons, we are constantly creating small ceremonies and celebrations to express both our inner feelings and our reactions to the world outside of us, celebrations to express delight and sorrow and anger, to say the least. It is this creating of small ceremonies and celebrations—rituals, if you will—that provides us with ways of unifying, maintaining, and transforming our experiences.

Arnold van Gennep, an anthropologist writing in the early 1900s, was among the first to note that rituals were a common and integrating phenomenon from almost the dawn of humankind; a way of saying yes to life's experiences. He saw that rituals were formed around three phases of dealing with human passage through life: separation, transition, and incorporation.[2]

A simple example is seen in the movement from childhood to adulthood. The individual separates from childhood, goes through a transition period, and is incorporated into adulthood. These movements have come to be known as the "rites of passage." In *Celebrate Life*, we refer to these as "milestones" and "times of transition or trauma."

In addition to the rituals developed to enable us to cope with making the passage from one phase of our lives into another, rituals were also developed to help us celebrate the passage from one phase of the calendar (seasonal cycles, religious cycles) into another.

Rituals Help Us Unify and Give Meaning to Life

Rituals begin by blazing an initial pathway into the unknown. Rituals then become an integrating, unifying, and ordering force to help people to bring the various threads of life together in such a way as to gain meaning and perspective, and to aid in the process of passage.

Say "hello," then shake hands—right hands. This is a greeting ritual that probably had its roots in the most primitive cultures when a stranger passed from one territory to another; the ritual provided the transition from uncertainty to certainty with regard to the stranger's intent. Since the right hand was considered the weapon hand, the handshake was then a disarming act and an example of a rite of passage.

Rituals Help Us Maintain and Transmit Our Faith

Rituals also provide the means of transmitting the faith from one generation to another. By "faith" we mean not only religious faith, but the faith of the culture, the etiquette, the social mores. These are the patterns of social behavior that make the difference between acceptance and rejection in the community. To provide this continuity and stability is the maintenance role of ritual.

In one culture, to burp at the end of a meal is the appropriate way of expressing appreciation to the cook. In another culture, the burp is a breach of etiquette, an insult. Thus is the ritual pattern of social behavior transmitted from generation to generation to maintain "appropriate" social customs and to protect the new generation from rejection.

Rituals Help Us Cope with Life

The old expression "Into every life some rain must fall" is a way of saying that all of us face difficulties and crises. Many of these are a normal part of the life cycle: birth, adolescence, illness, death. We are constantly faced with these crises. Rituals come into play to provide the "stuff" for reestablishing order in our lives in these times of trauma. They provide the breathing space necessary for individuals to cope with these crises and to once again say yes to life.

Our society, our particular community, our particular community of faith, all have established or traditional ways in which one is expected to deal with death, to grieve. To go through the established motions usually enables us to step back from the death, deal with the mundane, gain perspective and time before having to cope with the full consequences of the death. In other words, the ritual procedures are a means of helping us to cope and regain our ability to say yes to the living.

Rituals Help Us Transform Life

However, rituals do more than simply unify experiences; establish, maintain, and transmit order; and provide a means of coping with life. Rituals always have (or should always have) a transforming and liberating function. This function enables individuals and societies to change, to deal with new occasions. This function enables us to make the separation and the transition from the old and to incorporate the new.

James Russell Lowell, writing about the crisis our country faced in the
Civil War, said: "New occasions teach new duties; time makes ancient good
uncouth."[3] Paraphrasing, we might say, "New occasions call for new rituals.
Time makes old rituals obsolete." Thus, ritual helps blaze a new pathway into
the new unknown; it helps transform the new into established order.

In fact, it is this transforming and liberating function of ritual that ends up
being the most important function of all. This is what enables us to say yes to
life in all its aspects; to say yes to the power of the universe; to say yes to God.

For "if it be granted that we say yea to a single moment, then in so doing we
have said yea not only to ourselves, but to all existence."[4]

We Live in a Time of "Massive Ritual Boredom"

Unfortunately, rituals have fallen upon hard times—religious rituals in particular. Part of the reason for this is what Tom Driver calls "massive ritual
boredom," "a condition in which people have become fundamentally weary of
the rituals available to them for giving their lives shape and meaning." He
says: "Either the rituals, in their form, content, and manner of performance,
have lost touch with the actualities of people's lives and are thus simply
arcane; or else the people have lost the ability to apprehend their very need of
ritual, do not see what rituals are good for, and thus do not find them poten-
tially valuable."[5]

Somehow we have the feeling that the rituals we have no longer enable us
to say yes to life. They are not blazing new pathways into the unknown,
enabling us to unify the threads of our experiences and show us new meaning. They seem to have lost touch with our real lives.

Somehow we have the feeling that the rituals we have no longer enable us
to maintain and transmit our faith. Actually, we have the feeling that we have
no faith—no moral standards, no cultural standards. And because we seemingly have no faith to transmit, we have none to fall back on. Thus, we have
the feeling that the rituals we have no longer enable us to cope with life; they
no longer help us to say yes to living.

Probably no religious group is more appreciative of ritual than those of the
Jewish faith. They have significant home rituals related to the milestones and
times of passage in the lives of individuals and the family, as well as celebra-

tions of preparation for their corporate gatherings. Much of the underlying theological and sociological rationale for *Celebrate Life* owes its debt to these Jewish practices.

In one of their most significant celebrations, the Seder meal and service, Jewish people recount the events of the Passover and the Exodus from Egypt. It is truly an occasion of remembering. Over and over again, some aspect of the story of their bondage in Egypt and of God's deliverance is lifted up: word, song, symbol, food.

And yet, even within a tradition that values ritual, there is "massive ritual boredom" and a need for meaningful, transforming ritual. About three-fourths of the way through one Seder, a very bored, middle-aged gentleman was overheard to say, "If it was about the Holocaust, I could appreciate it, but this is deadly; deadly." The Central Conference of American Rabbis produced a Shabbat Manual, which opens with these words: "We know that Shabbat, as a discipline and as a source of noble living, has been lost to large numbers of our people, a loss which is both tragic and unnecessary. This Manual is our beginning in the effort to recover Shabbat observance as an enhancement of Jewish life, both for the individual Jew and for our people as a whole."[6]

We Live in a Time of Moral Emptiness

The loss of meaningful ritual actually has led to a sense of moral emptiness in our society. We are like ships without rudders. We sense that something is lost or that something is missing, but we do not seem to know what it is. To say that it is the loss of meaningful ritual is initially scoffed at, precisely because the rituals we have available to us are those for another time and place! The Exodus does not have as much relevance as does the Holocaust!

But if it is not the loss of meaningful ritual, what is it? For we continue to have a sense of moral emptiness, a dis-ease with the life around us! We wonder what has become of basic moral standards. All around us we witness the disintegration of traditional patterns of behavior in relationship to sex, other people, property, the law, and religion, to name but a few.

The patterns we see reflected in the life around us, on television, in the newspapers, in books and magazines, all seem to say that "anything goes!" Self-gratification seems to be the only criterion for behavior. Violence is the norm, not the exception. We begin to wonder how we will survive, no less how we might instill even the simplest values and patterns of behavior in our children! What can we do?

Tom Driver writes: "The desire for ritual seems to grow most urgent when people feel a prolonged or acute absence of moral guidance."[7] Some people are beginning to realize that it is very possible that the loss of meaningful ritual actually has led to this sense of moral emptiness in our society. In fact, a whole genre of books on ritual has developed in an attempt to fill this void in our lives.

Sensing the void, Sara Wenger Shenk compiled a book entitled *Why Not Celebrate!* She sought a way to enable her children to say yes to life; to say yes to God. A lengthy quote is appropriate:

> What values do I hold most dear? How do I tell my children who they are and where they fit into the vast array of cultures and religions? Either I pass these values on in a haphazard fashion, or I hand them to my children like priceless heirlooms, with care and forethought. Either I take my direction from the loudest, most current voices of the mass media, or I am nurtured by centuries of traditional stories and symbols which have guided countless families in prosperity and in adversity. . . .
>
> To create a structured family environment is to fashion a rhythm of meaningful activity so that a child can know safety and true freedom. Children need patterns and consistency in order to feel secure. There are so many changes in a child's larger world that he or she will receive great comfort from the reassuring repetition of memorable family celebrations. Children long for sameness, for the predictable return of a pleasurable experience. Like a cloak of security, repeated rituals surround a child with rhyme and reason, with anticipation and fulfillment, over and over again.[8]

One of the major problems that we run into in the attempt to create a "structured family environment" is that our family is more often separated than together. So often, the only time that whole families are together, under the same roof, doing the same thing, is when they are asleep at night.

"Celebratory Rituals for the Home" offers some suggestions, but there are really no easy answers. The first question, however, is probably the most important: Are we willing to make some drastic changes in our lives in order to establish new patterns of behavior for our new day, to transmit our faith to the next generation, and even to find some basis for our own affirmation of life? Unless we are willing to do this, our personal dis-ease with society will continue and so will the sense of moral emptiness pervading our land.

In the Shabbat Manual we referred to earlier, the rabbis make the same observation:

> Jews who have discarded Shabbat observance or Jews who have been deprived of it will not find it easy to reclaim all its treasures for themselves and their children. This Manual is a guide to these treasures. It is yours to use. We can only begin where we are. Each individual and each family will decide where and how to begin, and what and how much to do to make Shabbat an essential element in the rhythm of life. . . . The use of the following pages now depends on you.[9]

We Live in a Time of Rampant Individualism

Up to this point, we have stressed the need for meaningful rituals and their obvious loss in our society. We have indicated that a whole genre of literature on ritual has developed in an attempt to fill this void and to provide meaningful rituals for our day. Indeed, the first section of rituals tends to fit this mold.

However, *Celebrate Life* is also concerned with another significant loss in our society—the loss of a sense of community. From a religious perspective, it is the loss of a sense that our personal religious experience only has meaning when seen as a part of the corporate community of faith.

The modern classic study of American life, *Habits of the Heart,* clearly indicates that we live in a time of rampant individualism. This is so much so that the authors declare that as a result of their study: "We are concerned that this individualism may have grown cancerous."[10]

Individualism is the heartbeat of American society. The *Habits of the Heart* study says the following of our sense of individualism:

> We believe in the dignity, indeed the sacredness, of the individual. Anything that would violate our right to think for ourselves, judge for ourselves, make our own decisions, live our lives as we see fit, is not only morally wrong, it is sacrilegious. Our highest and noblest aspirations, not

only for ourselves, but for those we care about, for our society and for the world, are closely linked to our individualism. Yet, as we have been suggesting repeatedly in this book, some of our deepest problems both as individuals and as a society are also closely linked to our individualism.[11]

Individualism may be the heartbeat of American society, it is also the death knell of American society!

Our religious life clearly reflects the same situation. So often we have emphasized the need for our personal commitment to Jesus Christ, to have that inner experience of being born again, that we have lost the realization that such experiences take place not in isolation but in community—that is, they only have meaning in community! A simple example (and a truly sad one) is the practice of infant baptism as a private ceremony for the formal Christian naming of a child, rather than as a public, corporate celebration representing the birth of the child into the body of Christ, the family of God.

This emphasis on the personal nature of religious experience has resulted in most Christians finding it difficult to talk even to their children (never mind other to adults) about their own relationship to God. We are embarrassed by so-called God talk. Spirituality, our relationship to God and to the family of God, have all become more difficult than sex to discuss with our children.

In fact, this religious individualism has led to a true loss of understanding of our need to be with others in worship, to share our joys and our sorrows with one another, and to celebrate life together. We have lost the sense of corporateness, the sense of belonging to the larger community of faith. We have created a gap between what happens in our individual lives, what happens in our family, and what happens in church.

However, this gap goes both ways and for the same reasons. Individualism is rampant in our churches as well. The church has been more interested in maintaining itself as an institution and as a source of authority/power than it has been in supporting and empowering its members in their passage through life. Even when the concept of "the priesthood of all believers" has been espoused, its affirmation has been little more than lip service. To be a good member of the community of faith, of the church, too often simply means that one supports the church in its endeavor to survive.

The church's offices, its programs, and even its sacraments and rites, more often than not, are designed to maintain the status quo of the institution. By these very actions, the church, in effect, denies the corporate nature of its existence. It increases the gap between home and church.

Another example of the rampant individualism in our churches is seen in the growing emphasis on congregationalism, even in those churches that are episcopal in polity and structure. Individual congregations are growing more and more resentful of all outside authority. In so doing, the local church cuts itself off from the wider body to which it is connected in much the same way as individuals cut themselves off from the community of the church.

While many clergy have been affected by the liturgical movement and by the growing emphasis on the common lectionary, many have not, and most members of our churches seemingly couldn't care less. This reaction appears to be precisely because of the massive ritual boredom we have already mentioned. Thus, our individualism even cuts us off from a true sense of the wholeness and corporateness of the body of Christ.

Individualism may be the death knell of American society. It may also be the death knell of the church.

Ritual boredom, moral emptiness, rampant individualism—are these signs of an end time? Or signs of a between time?

"The Once and Future Church"

If Loren B. Mead, founder and president of the Alban Institute, is right, these are the signs of a between time. In his recent book *The Once and Future Church*, he describes the history of the church in a series of paradigms or patterns. Each paradigm or pattern develops in response to the church's understanding of its mission.[12]

One pattern emerged in response to the struggle to determine whether the church should be "identical to or different from its Jewish roots" and what its relationship should be to the Greco-Roman world. This pattern Mead calls the "paradigm of the apostolic age." Later, when Christianity became the official faith of the Roman Empire, Mead indicates that another significant reordering of the pattern took place. This reordering he calls the "paradigm of the age of Christendom."[13]

With each change of paradigm, roles and relationships change and power shifts. New structures develop. New directions emerge. Things that were of great value in one age become useless in the next. Times of transition between ages and paradigms are times of confusion and tumult. And, in our own time, that second paradigm is breaking apart. Its successor—a third paradigm—has yet to appear fully.[14]

We have to agree with Mead that ritual boredom, moral emptiness, and rampant individualism are the signs of a time when the old is breaking apart and the new is not yet apparent. We are in one of those traumatic and turbulent times that van Gennep called a time of transition, a between time.

In this between time, we offer *Celebrate Life* in the hope that it will serve as a means for us to blaze new pathways into the unknown future, integrating, unifying, and ordering our lives. We hope that it may serve as a means for us to transmit our faith to our children.

In this between time, we offer *Celebrate Life* in the hope that it will serve as a means to end our ritual boredom and fill our moral emptiness. We hope that it will serve as a means to bridge the gap between our individualism and our sense of corporateness (especially our sense of the corporateness of our faith) and that it may serve as a means to bridge the gap between home and church.

In this between time, we offer *Celebrate Life* in the hope that it may serve as a means and not as an end!

Celebratory Rituals for the

Home

There can be no question about the importance of the meal table as a focus of religious and social significance in the ancient Near East. J. Jeremias expresses the point well:

> To invite a man to a meal was an honour. It was an offer of peace, trust, brotherhood and forgiveness; in short, sharing a table meant sharing life. . . .
>
> In Judaism in particular, table-fellowship means fellowship before God, for the eating of a piece of broken bread by everyone who shares in the meal brings out the fact that they all have a share in the blessing which the master of the house had spoken over the unbroken bread.

This, what we might call the sacredness of the meal table, is often lost sight of in a Christianity where the link between sacrament and meal has been long broken and the heightened sacredness of the sacrament has resulted in a diminished religious significance for the ordinary meal.

—*James D. G. Dunn*[1]

The Home

The multiplicity of the forms of family life today creates a real problem when trying to define "family," "home," or even "family values." Without arguing the pros and cons of various definitions, in *Celebrate Life* we understand "family" to mean those with whom we relate in a significant manner, and "home" to mean where the family gathers.

We all relate to someone, hopefully in a significant manner. We call that relationship "family." This concept of family has its basis in an excellent article by John Patton in *The Christian Century* magazine several years ago. He wrote:

> We need a theological norm for family living that emphasizes family function rather than family form. For those who have never married, who are separated, divorced or widowed can also have a family life. I suggest we understand Christian family living to mean relating seriously and caringly to persons in the generation of one's parents, to those in one's own generation, and to the generations of children and grandchildren which carry the family into the future. The quality of care for family members in one's own generation and in the generations before and after is more important than the form or structure of one's household. In fact, this norm of caring for the generations can apply . . . to all sorts and conditions of human beings.[2]

Using this definition of "family," we can have a wide variety of forms while having one basic function: that of relating seriously and caringly to others. We would like to think that these forms may include individuals who are not related by blood or marriage—that a family may even consist of neighbors.

We all live somewhere. The family gathers somewhere. We call this "home."

The Home Gathering

We have indicated that one of the major problems facing the family is that it is more often separated than together. In the midst of this pattern of separation, anyone who is concerned about providing the home with a structured family environment is faced with real difficulties.

However, if we feel that it is important for our own mental health, for helping us to cope with life, and for both the establishment and transmission of our family values, then a serious commitment must be made to providing our family with time for what we call a "home gathering." The home gathering provides the basis for a structured family environment.

Some traditional and/or nuclear families may find it possible to have a home gathering daily, around the evening meal or around the children's bedtime. Other families may find such a schedule impossible.

Some families may determine that there is one particular day in the week that is best for them to have a home gathering. For example, it is traditional for Jewish families to gather each Friday evening in preparation for the Sabbath, in what is known as the Shabbat dinner and celebration. A Christian family may find that holding the home gathering on a Saturday evening is a very appropriate and meaningful way to prepare for the coming together of the larger family, the church gathering.

Other families may find that even a weekly home gathering is just not possible. They may feel that a monthly home gathering is all that their family schedule allows.

The point is that the family must decide to make a commitment to providing for some structured environment and must set the way or ways this is to take place. However and whenever the family has a home gathering, the key is to give absolute priority to it!

The home gathering is the focal point of all the suggested ritual celebrations for the family. It is the activity that provides continuity and stability. It is the pattern, the ritual, that helps unify all that the family is and believes. The home gathering is to be used not only to mark the milestones and times of joy, transition, or trauma in the lives of family members, but also to prepare for the celebrations of the community of faith. Thus, the home gathering will provide the needed corrective to the individualism of our day; it will tie us to the corporate body of Christ; it will help bridge the gap between home and church.

Craig D. Erickson, in *Participating in Worship*, stresses this type of bridging through the emphasis on lay leadership in worship—both home worship (home gathering) and corporate worship (church gathering). He writes:

It is in the home where Lay Leadership in worship is most needed. A sim-
plified form of Morning and Evening Prayer (from the Divine Office) provides a structure for family devotional activity. There are many advan-
tages to this pattern, not the least of which is the obvious inter-
relationship of household, subcongregational, and festival celebrations of
Morning and Evening Prayer. When household devotions follow the patterns for Morning and Evening Prayer, they manifest their tie to the corporate prayer of the church, much as table grace before meals resonates
with the Eucharistic Prayer.[3]

Having regular home gatherings provides repetitive behavior patterns so
that the celebrations of the milestones and the times of joy, transition, or
trauma are seen as a regular part of the life of the family, and not just as "add-
ons" for some special occasion. This regular routine provides the stabilizing
strength of the ritual gathering and serves as a tool for transmitting family
values and faith.

The Home Gathering Symbol

Even as the home gathering is the focal point of all the celebrations, so we
suggest that each family choose a symbol to serve as the focus for all home
gatherings. We suggest that because these are celebrations of the Christian
home, this central symbol should reflect the conviction of the family that
Christ is the Sovereign of this particular home. The symbol thus will become
a constant reminder that Christ is the unseen presence for all that is said and
done in the home. It also becomes a silent witness to all who enter the home
that Christ is the Sovereign of all life there.

Jack Lundin, in *Celebrations for Special Days and Occasions,* describes how
his family decided to use a family cup of blessing as central to all of their
family celebrations.[4] He explains that the cup has a great deal of teaching
value as it relates to Jewish history and to the Eucharist, or Holy Communion. His book is most helpful to anyone seeking to develop variations or
additions to the suggestions in *Celebrate Life.*

Another family symbol might be a cross that has particular meaning or significance to the family. It may have been carved by a friend. It may have been
created by a child. It may be a special gift.

The Home Gathering Setting Used in Celebrate Life

The generic home family in *Celebrate Life* has determined to hold its home gatherings on Saturday evenings in order to better prepare for the church gathering. The family has made a commitment to eat the evening meal together on that day and to hold the home gathering as a part of the meal. In addition, the family has decided to begin each evening meal eaten at home by lighting the candle and offering a blessing, and to end those meals with a closing blessing and extinguishing the candle.

The generic home family in *Celebrate Life* has chosen to use a home gathering centerpiece which is placed in the dining room. The centerpiece consists of a round board, with appropriate-sized holes drilled into it to allow for the placing of four Advent candles and a small dowel stick on which various symbols of the liturgical church year are placed. The main symbol is a large candle, which represents Christ as the light of the world. The centerpiece is changed with each change in the church year. The centerpiece components for each season are:

Advent season: A large white Christ candle surrounded by an Advent wreath with violet or blue Advent candles. The Advent candle is to be lit on the appropriate Sundays during Advent, and the center candle each night the rest of the week.

Christmas season: A large white Christ candle and crèche figures, or a small crèche scene with candles.

Epiphany and the time following: A large white Christ candle with an Epiphany star behind it or the crèche figures with the magi added.

Lenten season: A large violet/purple candle with a cross behind it.

Easter season: A large white Christ candle with a butterfly behind it or the cross with a butterfly on it.

Pentecost and the time following: A large green candle with a dove behind it. Since this is a very long season, the centerpiece can be decorated with various flowers, items gathered from family trips, etc.

The Christ candle remains constant throughout the year, serving this family as a silent reminder that "Christ is the light of the world. Christ is the light of our lives."

A number of the rituals suggest the use a plate with the words "You Are Special" on it. See if you can find something similar in a local card or gift shop.

For other rituals, it is recommended that you use a "broken"cross—one that can be taken apart and put back together again. This can be the same cross that is used regularly, if it is so designed.

Your Family and Celebrate Life

Once you and your family have made a commitment to hold regular home gathering celebrations, you will need to determine when these shall take place, what you will use as your home gathering symbol, and what basic pattern you will follow. We do suggest that you use the home gathering as presented here several times before beginning to adopt your own particular pattern.

Check your local religious bookstore for intergenerational, lectionary-based devotions for use at home. *The New Century Hymnal*[5] provides an evening prayer service and a large number of other resources that can be used in the home. See the additional resources listed at the end of this book for some more suggested aids for helping your family develop its own celebrations.

We must reiterate that the home gathering celebration and all of the celebratory rituals in *Celebrate Life* are only suggested guides for you to use in the development of your own family rituals and celebrations. When you do develop your own, you might bear in mind the guidelines offered by Tom F. Driver. He suggests that the ritual should take place at a particular time, utilizing a designated space and following a particular rhythm, and should consist of specific actions all designed to celebrate, to say yes to some word of life and faith.[6]

Each ritual you develop should try to include as many of the senses as possible. They should be flexible, freeing, ordering, joyous, transforming, God/Christ-centered, Spirit-infused, and should serve as a bridge between home and church wherever possible.

Enjoy! Celebrate! Celebrate life!

The Basic Home Gathering

It is suggested that you use the basic home gathering as it appears here several times before either adapting it for your own particular family or using one of the other celebratory rituals. The home family in *Celebrate Life* for every evening meal uses only the lighting of the candles, the blessing, and the extinguishing of the candles; they use the whole home gathering only on Saturday evenings.

The Lighting of the Candles

Before the meal, a family member usually lights the candles. A gracious gesture of Christian hospitality would be to ask a guest to light the candles. As the candles are lit, say:

All: Christ is the light of the world. Christ is the light of our lives.

The Blessing

Take turns breaking the bread. If the home gathering is not held at mealtime, then eliminate this blessing.

All: In praise of you, O God, we break this bread (*break a piece of bread*), for by your gracious love we all are fed. Amen.

Share bread with all present.

The Song of Celebration

After the meal, sing or play a hymn, a children's song, or other music appropriate for the occasion. For example, you may wish to sing this song:

> Rise, shine, give God the glory, glory,
> Rise and shine and give God the glory, glory,
> Rise and shine and (*clap*) give God the glory, glory,
> Children of our God.

> —*Old Spiritual*

The Reading of the Word

At a meal:

All: As our bodies have been fed, O God, now feed our souls on your Word of life.

At other times:

All: May the light of your Word illumine our hearts.

Read a passage of scripture you find most appropriate. Selections from the *Revised Common Lectionary* for the coming Sunday are excellent choices, particularly if your church uses the lectionary regularly.

The Spoken Response

All: Let your Word abide in us, O God.

The Sung Response

Sing a hymn of your own choosing or use the following:

> Hallelu, hallelu, hallelu, hallelujah! Praise ye the Lord!
> For the light of your Word, and our gath'ring together, praise ye the Lord.
> Praise ye the Lord, hallelujah! Praise ye the Lord, hallelujah!
> Praise ye the Lord, hallelujah! Praise ye the Lord!

> *—Traditional; words of second line by Peter Young, 1995*

The Sharing

A family thanks-offering box, hunger appeal box, Lenten coin folder, or other church appeal container may be made an integral part of the centerpiece. *Place gifts in the container.*

Leader: Happy are those who consider the poor.

The Period of Prayer

Families often find it helpful to stand and join hands. A short period of silence followed by one-sentence prayers by each person present is very meaningful and is a very useful training tool for children. Prayers of thanksgiving and/or intercession for others should be encouraged. Older children should take turns ending with a closing prayer, which may be extemporaneous or may use the following prayer, designed to make the family conscious of the church gathering the next day.

All: We praise and thank you, O God, that you have not left us alone in this world. We thank you that we do not have to rely on our own strength or resources. You have called us to be part of the community of faith, the church, our church. You have called us to be members one of another, with all who share in the resurrection faith. You have called us to worship and to serve as one in the body of Christ. Prepare our hearts for this worship and service. Blessed be your name, O God, forever and ever. Amen.

The Blessing

In families with children present, this is most meaningful.

Parents place their hands on the heads of the children.

Parents: May you love God, love yourself, and love your neighbor. May you walk always in the light and love of Jesus Christ.

Children hold hands with their parents.

Children: May our love for one another grow stronger day by day.

All: Amen.

If no children are present, everyone may say the blessing:

All: God bless you and take care of you. God be kind and gracious to you. God look on you with favor and give you peace. Amen.[7]

The Extinguishing of the Candles

Leader: May the shalom, the peace of God, enfold us as the shadows of the night descend upon us.

All: Amen.

··· The Dedication of the Home Gathering Symbol ···

Place the home gathering centerpiece and candle in a central location (for example, on the dining room table). Place the various symbols of the church year you will be using around the centerpiece. Have the family gather around, hold hands in silence, and then join in this or a similar dedication.

Leader: Blessed God, we place this candle in the center of our home.

All: For you are the center of all life.

Leader: Blessed God, we dedicate this candle that it may be a sign of the unity of our life together as a family.

All: For you are the giver of all life.

Leader: Blessed God, we pray that our gathering together in times of joy and of sorrow may deepen the ties of love in our life together.

All: For you have given us one another to provide support and caring in the midst of life.

Leader: Blessed God, may all who join our circle from time to time find love and peace here.

All: For you are the source of all love and peace.

Leader: Blessed God, we surround this candle with the symbols of the larger family to which we belong.

All: For you have given us the church to strengthen and nourish us for service in the world.

Leader: Blessed God, we light this candle (*light the candle*).

All: For Christ is the light of the world. Christ is the light of our lives. Amen.

···Home Gathering Rituals···

The home gathering rituals included on the following pages are divided into the following general categories: times of new life, times of growth, times of significant change, times of uncertainty, times of significant loss, times of separation, times of special concern, times related to our faith journey and church life, and celebrations of preparation for the church gathering.

You will find examples of various rituals designed to bridge the gap between home and church. Utilize the home gathering framework for these celebrations, but make each celebration special in itself. In celebrating milestones, times of joy, and times of transition, be free, flexible, and joyous. In commemorating times of trauma, adhering to the basic home gathering ceremony will help bring order and stability; it will give the breathing space necessary for coping with the trauma. The candle-lighting and blessing rituals before the meal are not repeated for each celebration; they are given only where something special is suggested. Remember, develop what is meaningful for you and your family.

In most of the rituals, we have not mentioned special foods; however, in many cultures and in many families, certain foods play a very important role in the celebration. You are encouraged to make some particular food special to your own celebrations as you develop your own family traditions.

Times of New Life

··· Engagement or Marriage ···

The time of an engagement or a pending marriage is a wonderful time for the couple and their families to gather for a celebratory meal, to open communication between the families, and to share in home gathering together. In preparation for this home gathering, members of the family may wish to bring some component to be used for a home gathering centerpiece to offer to the couple during the celebration.

The Song of Celebration

At the conclusion of the meal, gather in a circle and sing a couple of joyful songs, family favorites. You may wish to use the following.

JOIN MAN AND WOMAN (TO THE TUNE OF "MORNING HAS BROKEN")

1. Join man and woman In holy wedlock,
   Two that are different Two shall be one.
   Praise for the union Out of commitment.
   Pledged to each other And to their God.

2. Pour out the spirit Of true compassion,
   Bind them together In your great love.
   Praise for the children Born of this spirit,
   Bless this sweet family, Heavenly Dove.

3. Praise to the Maker, And to the Spirit,
   Praise to the Savior, Our triune God.
   Praise for God's blessings Poured out upon us.
   Praise for this couple Now joined as one.

—Peter Young, 1982

The Reading of the Word

After a meal:

All: As our bodies have been fed, O God, now feed our souls on your Word of life.

At other times:

All: May the light of your Word illumine our hearts.

A suggested passage for this celebration is 1 Corinthians 13.

The Spoken Response

All: Let your Word abide in us, O God.

The Sung Response

Sing a hymn of your own choosing or use the following:

Hallelu, hallelu, hallelu, hallelujah! Praise ye the Lord!
For the light of your Word, and our gath'ring together, praise ye
   the Lord!
Praise ye the Lord, hallelujah! Praise ye the Lord, hallelujah!
Praise ye the Lord, hallelujah! Praise ye the Lord!

—Traditional; words of second line by Peter Young, 1995

The Period of Prayer and Sharing

At this point, we suggest that you ask the engaged couple to step into the center of the circle. Let each person then offer a prayer as a "toast," to which everyone responds with the words "So be it!" Following each prayer, the person may wish to present the couple with one part of a home gathering centerpiece: a base, a candle, a cross, or the like.

The Blessing

While still in this circle with the couple in the center, all place their hands on the heads of the couple.

All: May Christ be at the center of your lives, even as you are in the center of the circle of our lives. Amen.

The Extinguishing of the Candles
Return to the table.

All: May the shalom, the peace of God, enfold us as the shadows of
             the night descend upon us. Amen.

Sit around the table and share times of joy and sorrow as you reminisce about
the past in the lives of the couple and in both families.

···Pregnancy···

You may wish to place a pair of baby shoes or some similar item on the home
gathering centerpiece to symbolize the joy of this occasion. We also suggest
that where there are other children in the family, you light one candle for
each child and the Christ candle.

The Song of Celebration
Sing a hymn of your own choosing or use the following, sung to the tune of
"Whisper a Prayer":

> We offer our thanks in the morning,
> We offer our thanks at noon,
> We offer our thanks in the evening,
> For a new life that's coming so soon.

The Reading of the Word
After a meal:

All: As our bodies have been fed, O God, now feed our souls on your
             Word of life.

At other times:

All: May the light of your Word illumine our hearts.

A good scripture for the occasion is Luke 1:46–55.

The Spoken Response

All: Let your Word abide in us, O God.

The Sung Response

Sing a hymn of your own choosing or use the following:

> Hallelu, hallelu, hallelu, hallelujah! Praise ye the Lord!
> For the light of your Word, and our gath'ring together, praise ye
>   the Lord!
> Praise ye the Lord, hallelujah! Praise ye the Lord, hallelujah!
> Praise ye the Lord, hallelujah! Praise ye the Lord!

> *—Traditional; words of second line by Peter Young, 1995*

The Sharing

Make a special gift to an organization dedicated to the welfare of children.

The Period of Prayer

We are indebted to Jack W. Lundin, *Celebrations for Special Days and Occasions,* for the following prayer.

All members of the family place their hands on the mother's abdomen.

Husband and wife: An act of love was and now is and will become by a grace
            beyond us! O God, we feel the gift of life, a secret made to be
            ours, and we are grateful. May your love for us and your trust in
            our impending parenthood be noted this day by us both. We
            humbly accept your grace. Make us sensitive to your gift.

All: Amen.[8]

In families where there are other children, this may be a good time to discuss how each person feels about the new family member soon to be born. This will help the children to express their particular concerns about the effect this new child will have on their own lives.

The Blessing

You may wish to alter this blessing to reflect any concerns the children in the family may have expressed in the above conversation.

Parents place their hands on the heads of the children.

Parents: May you love God, love yourself, and love your neighbor. May you love the new life growing in our midst and welcome the new member of our family when he or she is born. May you walk always in the light of Jesus Christ.

Children hold hands with their parents.

Children: May our love for one another and for the new life in our midst grow stronger day by day.

All: Amen.

If no children are present, everyone may say the blessing:

All: God bless you and take care of you. God be kind and gracious to you. God look on you with favor and give you peace. Amen.

The Extinguishing of the Candles

Leader: May the shalom, the peace of God, enfold us as the shadows of the night descend upon us.

All: Amen.

··· Birth or Adoption ···

We suggest that this particular celebration be held after the meal on the day when the child arrives home for the first time. As with the celebration of pregnancy, we suggest that where there are other children in the family, you light a candle for each family member.

The Welcoming of the Child into the Home

The father holds up the child for all to see. If an adopted child is old enough, he or she can stand on a chair.

Mother: We welcome *(child's name)* into our home.

Eldest child: Welcome, little brother/sister.

Younger child: Welcome in love.

Youngest child: Welcome in joy.

All: Welcome to our home. Come, see your new home.

The Song of Celebration

Sing "He's Got the Whole World in His Hands" as you parade from room to room. Show the child a room, sing one verse of the song, say something about the use of the room (for example, "This is where we eat and play games together," "This is where you will sleep," etc.). Then return to the table.

The Reading of the Word

After a meal:

All: As our bodies have been fed, O God, now feed our souls on your Word of life.

At other times:

All: May the light of your Word illumine our hearts.

Possible scriptures for the occasion are Luke 1:46–55 or Psalm 8 or Psalm 150.

The Spoken Response

All: Let your Word abide in us, O God.

The Sung Response

Sing a hymn of your own choosing or use the following:

Hallelu, hallelu, hallelu, hallelujah! Praise ye the Lord!
For the light of your Word, and our gath'ring together, praise ye
   the Lord!
Praise ye the Lord, hallelujah! Praise ye the Lord, hallelujah!
Praise ye the Lord, hallelujah! Praise ye the Lord!

—Traditional; words of second line by Peter Young, 1995

The Sharing

We suggest that a small gift be given to each of the older children from the baby or new family member, and that each child give a gift in return. This exchange is particularly meaningful if the gift is not a toy, but rather some token that will remind the recipient of this special day (for example, a plaque, a picture made for the occasion, etc.).

The Period of Prayer

We suggest one-sentence prayers of thanksgiving from each member of the family.

The Blessing

Parents place their hands on the heads of the children.

Parents: May you love God, love yourself, and love your neighbor. May you walk always in the light of Jesus Christ.

Children hold hands with their parents.

Children: May our love for one another grow stronger day by day.

All: Amen.

The Extinguishing of the Candles

Let each person extinguish a candle representative of himself or herself, and then let a parent or the older adopted child conclude.

Parent or adoptive child: May the shalom, the peace of God, enfold us as the darkness of night descends upon us.

All: Amen.

··· New Grandchild ···

It is assumed that this celebration will take place in the absence of any members of the family other than the grandparent(s). If there are any other grandchildren in the family, place pictures of them around the home gathering centerpiece. Also place there a picture of the new parents and a picture of the new grandchild (if one is available).

The Song of Celebration

We suggest that you sing "Let Us with a Gladsome Mind," by John Milton. This is found in most hymnals. The following verse, by Peter Young (1991), may be used as a new verse 4, with the present verse 4 becoming verse 5:

> Blessed new life God has given, Grandchild sweet, a bit of heaven:
> For God's mercies shall endure, Ever faithful, ever sure.

The Reading of the Word

After a meal:

All: As our bodies have been fed, O God, now feed our souls on your Word of life.

At other times:

All: May the light of your Word illumine our hearts.

Possible scriptures for the occasion are Psalm 78:1–8, Psalm 150, or Ecclesiastes 3:1–8.

The Spoken Response

All: Let your Word abide in us, O God.

The Sung Response

Sing a hymn of your own choosing or use the following:

> Hallelu, hallelu, hallelu, hallelujah! Praise ye the Lord!
> For the light of your Word, and our gath'ring together, praise ye
>   the Lord!
> Praise ye the Lord, hallelujah! Praise ye the Lord, hallelujah!
> Praise ye the Lord, hallelujah! Praise ye the Lord!

> *—Traditional; words of second line by Peter Young, 1995*

The Sharing

We suggest that each grandparent write a letter to the new grandchild. Share with the child your thoughts and feelings on this day of celebration. Share also your hopes and dreams for the child.

The Period of Prayer

The grandparents take turns holding up family pictures, beginning with one of the new parents. Then they offer a prayer of thanksgiving and blessing for each member of the family. You may wish to conclude with this special prayer or one of your own.

Grandparents: Miracle of miracles, a new life has come into our midst. We pray that the grace and mercy of God, the love and peace of Christ, and the strength and presence of the Spirit will always be with our beloved grandchild. Amen.

The Blessing

Grandparents: God bless you and take care of you. God be kind and gracious to you. God look on you with favor and give you peace. God watch over this newest member of our family. Amen.

The Extinguishing of the Candles

Grandparents: May the shalom, the peace of God, enfold us and our loved ones as the shadows of the night descend upon us. Amen.

Times of Growth

··· A First Coming of Age ···

The time when a child moves from the crib to a bed is, in a real sense, a first coming of age. It is also a time of separation. It is joyful, and it is traumatic. On the day your family has its home gathering celebration to mark this first coming of age, you may wish to use the "You Are Special" plate or your family equivalent, to indicate the specialness of the occasion. The child should be helped to light the candle and break the bread at the beginning of the home gathering. If the child is to receive a new bed and is old enough, he or she should be involved in the decision-making process. Let the child shop with you for the bed. Have the new bed ready to assemble.

The Lighting of the Candles
(Prior to the meal.)

> Christ is the Light of the world.
> Christ is the Light of our lives.

All: In praise of you, O God, we break this bread *(break a piece of bread),* for by your gracious love we all are fed. Amen. *(Share bread with all present.)*

The Extinguishing of the Candles
(Following the conclusion of the meal ceremony.)

Leader: May the shalom, the peace of God, enfold us as the shadows of the night descend upon us.

All: Amen.

Move to the bedroom for the completion of the celebration.

The Song of Celebration
We suggest that you sing the familiar "Twinkle, Twinkle, Little Star," and then, as you stand by the crib, end with these words:

How I love you, little crib,
Thank you for the things you did.
You made me feel safe and sound,
Warm and cozy all around.
Now I leave you, little crib,
Thank you for the things you did.

—*Peter Young, 1993*

The Reading of the Word
After a meal:
All: As our bodies have been fed, O God, now feed our souls on your Word of life.
At other times:
All: May the light of your Word illumine our hearts.
A good scripture to use is Matthew 19:13–15.

The Spoken Response
All: Let your Word abide in us, O God.

The Sung Response
Sing a hymn of your own choosing or use the following:

Hallelu, hallelu, hallelu, hallelujah! Praise ye the Lord!
For the light of your Word, and our gath'ring together, praise ye
   the Lord!
Praise ye the Lord, hallelujah! Praise ye the Lord, hallelujah!
Praise ye the Lord, hallelujah! Praise ye the Lord!

—*Traditional; words of second line by Peter Young, 1995*

The Act of Transition and Prayer

Dismantle the crib, and assemble the new bed. Allow the child to help. Give the child a new bedspread to place on the bed. Have him or her add a favorite item from the crib (for example, a blanket, a pillow, or a toy).

Parent: Loving God, we thank you for the growing that takes place in our lives. It is always so good to move on to new things, to new experiences. And yet, it is always hard when moving on means leaving behind. As *(child's name)* moves on to this new bed, may it be a time of joy and excitement. May s/he realize that this is another step in growing up, and may s/he always remember that you are with her/him in all new times and places.

All: Amen.

The Blessing

Parents place their hands on the heads of the children.

Parents: May you love God, love yourself, and love your neighbor. May you walk always in the light of Jesus Christ.

Children hold hands with their parents.

Children: May our love for one another grow stronger day by day.

All: Amen.

Join hands and sing "Taps":

> Day is done, gone the sun
> From the lake, from the hill, from the sky;
> All is well, safely rest; God is nigh.

> —Traditional

··· Birthday ···

Most families have their own traditional ways of celebrating birthdays, but if you have not already established some traditions, you may wish to include this suggestion in your home gathering celebration. If you have a "You Are Special" plate, this would be a good time to use it. If you do not have the plate, we suggest that you use something similar to designate the special person to be honored at this celebration. If the celebration is for a child and the child is old enough, have him or her light the candle and break the bread.

The Celebration
Everyone loves a parade! While the special person remains at the table, clear the table by parading to the kitchen, carrying the dishes and singing:

> Skidamarink a dink a dink, skidamarink a doo, I love you.
> Skidamarink a dink a dink, skidamarink a doo, I love you.
> I love you in the morning and in the afternoon,
> I love you in the evening and underneath the moon, oh,
> Skidamarink a dink a dink, skidamarink a doo, I love you.

> *—Traditional*

As you continue to march around the dining room table, gather up the special person, and then parade throughout the house, continuing to sing. Having placed gifts in various rooms prior to the celebration, shower the special person with them as you parade. Complete the circuit through the kitchen, picking up the birthday cake and any other items for the party. Then return to the table and place the cake in front of the honoree.

Mother: It is a special day in the life of (*person's name*), and we are privileged to share in the celebration of this birthday. To you we all say:

All: Happy birthday, (*person's name*)!

Father: In celebrating this special day, we give thanks to God for allow-
                 ing us the privilege of being a part of (*person's name*)'s family. We
                 open our hearts to a favorite passage from God's Word.

Read celebrant's favorite passage or Psalm 139:1–6, 13–18.

Mother: We give thanks to God for all that (*person's name*) means to each
                 one of us.

*Each person present calls out the honoree's relationship to him or her (for
example, son, daughter, sister, brother, cousin, friend, grandchild). For older
children and adults, you may wish to do more than simply call out the relationship. Everyone present may wish to share a brief story or event related to the
honoree that is particularly meaningful to them, or explain why they are happy
to share in this celebration. This is also an appropriate point in the celebration
to offer one-sentence prayers for the individual.*

Siblings: May the joy and the love we share this day make each day in the
                 year ahead brighter and more beautiful. Do you agree?

All: Yes! Yes! Yes!

Sing "Happy Birthday."

The Blessing

Form a circle with the honoree in the center.

All: May you love God, love yourself, and love your neighbor as we
                 love you. May you walk always in the light of Jesus Christ.

Honoree: May our love for one another grow stronger day by day.

All: Amen.

The Extinguishing of the Candles

Where age-appropriate, have the honoree lead.

Leader: May the shalom, the peace of God, enfold us as the shadows of
                 the night descend upon us.

All: Amen.

··· Coming of Age (Adolescence) ···

Probably one of the most significant events in an individual's life is the onset of puberty. Most cultures have developed some type of puberty or coming-of-age rite. This is particularly true of those societies that are more communally oriented than our own. We, in the United States and possibly in most Western societies, have lost that sense of community, and in so doing, have lost true coming-of-age rituals. A family needs to determine for itself when it feels a given child has come of age. The emphasis in this particular celebration is on coming of age itself rather than on any specific event. This is another occasion when you may wish to use a "You Are Special" plate. In preparation, ask the young person being honored to bring a special childhood toy to the home gathering. She or he may be invited to light the candle and break the bread.

The Ritual of Passage

Father: *(Youth's name)*, please stand away from the table. Hear these words of the apostle Paul: "When I was a child, I thought like a child, I spoke like a child, I reasoned like a child; when I became an adult, I put an end to childish ways" (1 Cor. 13:11). *(Youth's name)*, are you ready to put away childish ways?

Youth: I am.

Mother: As a sign that you are indeed ready to put away childish ways, take one of your special toys, leave the house, and return without it.

The toy may be given to another child or disposed of in some appropriate manner, but in such a way that it is no longer the property of the youth. This should be arranged for in advance so that the young person is not away long.

Youth: I have put away childish things.

The Song of Celebration

We suggest you sing "Lonesome Valley":

> Jesus walk'd this lonesome valley, He had to walk it by himself,
> Oh, nobody else could walk it for him, He had to walk it by himself.

We must walk this lonesome valley, We have to walk it by ourselves,
Oh, nobody else can walk it for us, We have to walk it by ourselves.

You must walk the lonesome valley, You must walk it by yourself,
Oh, nobody else can walk it for you, You have to walk it by yourself.

—Traditional; third verse by Peter Young, 1994

The Ritual of Passage Continues

Father: Having put away childish things, we invite you to take up the journey to full adulthood. There are many lonesome valleys ahead. There are many times when you will yearn to be a child again. While the decisions are yours to make, so are the consequences of those decisions, for good or for ill.

Mother: This time is as moving and as frightening for us as it is for you. It is difficult for us, as your parents, to let you walk alone. Yet, as we let you go, it would not be right for us to let you think that our letting go means that we no longer care.

Father: We care. And we will be there as one adult for the other. We will be there for you with our love and support, not to do for you, but to help you to do for yourself. Are you ready to take the next step?

Youth: I am.

Father (to son) or mother (to daughter): Then come back to the table and sit in my place (*parent and youth exchange seats*).

The Sharing

An appropriate gift, symbolic of the coming of age, should be given by the parents at this time.

The Period of Prayer

Join hands around the table. After a short period of silence, a prayer should be offered by the one who is coming of age.

The Blessing

The normal blessing of all the children is eliminated tonight, as the other children should remain as inconspicuous as possible. Their time will come, or has already come.

The Extinguishing of the Candles

The one who is coming of age extinguishes the candles.

All: May the shalom, the peace of God, enfold us as the shadows of the night descend upon us. Amen.

···Gay or Lesbian Identity (Coming Out)···

This ritual is designed to help the family of an individual who has come to know that he or she is gay or lesbian and who has expressed this understanding to the family. It is both a "You Are Special" plate and a wooden cross occasion. The plate expresses the specialness of the individual. The broken cross, which can be taken apart and put back together again, expresses the inner turmoil the individual has gone through in determining his or her sexual orientation. Have the cross taken apart before you begin the ritual.

The Song of Celebration

A suggested hymn is "I Sing the Mighty Power of God." It would also be appropriate to choose the person's favorite hymn.

The Reading of the Word

After a meal:

All: As our bodies have been fed, O God, now feed our souls on your Word of life.

At other times:

All: May the light of your Word illumine our hearts.

Some suggested readings are Genesis 1:1–2:4 and John 3:1–17.

The Spoken Response

All: Let your Word abide in us, O God.

The Sung Response

Sing a hymn of your own choosing or use the following:

> Hallelu, hallelu, hallelu, hallelujah! Praise ye the Lord!
>
> For the light of your Word, and our gath'ring together, praise ye the Lord!
>
> Praise ye the Lord, hallelujah! Praise ye the Lord, hallelujah!
>
> Praise ye the Lord, hallelujah! Praise ye the Lord!

—Traditional; words of second line by Peter Young, 1995

The Sharing

This is the time for some honest sharing of feelings and concerns by the whole family. The person who has just come out leads.

Leader: I would like to share with you . . .

The person expresses the feelings that he or she experienced before and after coming out. They may range from confusion, fear, living a lie, and feeling "different," to relief, pride, and self-acceptance.

Family member: I would like to respond by sharing with you . . .

Each person present expresses his or her own feelings—positive and negative— about the family member's coming out.

The Period of Prayer

One family member joins the pieces of the broken cross.

Leader: That God so loved the world, meaning each one of us, is expressed by the cross of Christ. It was through this cross that God took all broken relationships and made them whole. It is because of this act of love that we now turn to God in prayer.

Each person offers an individual prayer growing out of the sharing and the concerns expressed. They conclude by praying in unison the Prayer of Our Savior.

The Blessing

With the person in the center of circle, all place their hands on his or her head.

All: God bless you and take care of you. God be kind and gracious to you. God look on you with favor and give you peace. Amen.

The Extinguishing of the Candles
The person acts as leader.
Leader: May the shalom, the peace and wholeness of God enfold us as
                 the shadows of the night descend upon us.
All: Amen.

···Graduation···

A graduation, even from kindergarten, is an opportunity for remembering and celebrating. It represents a milestone in one's life. Most graduates have some type of party, which usually includes the friends of the graduate. We suggest that the home gathering celebration be held at a time separate from such a party and that it include only members of the immediate family and relatives. We offer two possible ways of marking this time of growth. Incorporate these suggestions into your regular home gathering wherever you feel they are most appropriate. Use a "You Are Special" plate.

The Song of Celebration
Sing one of the graduate's favorite songs or hymns.

The Reading of the Word
After a meal:
All: As our bodies have been fed, O God, now feed our souls on your
                 Word of life.
At other times:
All: May the light of your Word illumine our hearts.
Read the graduate's favorite passage of scripture.

The Spoken Response
All: Let your Word abide in us, O God.

The Sung Response

Sing a hymn of your own choosing or use the following:

> Hallelu, hallelu, hallelu, hallelujah! Praise ye the Lord!
> For the light of your Word, and our gath'ring together, praise ye
>   the Lord!
> Praise ye the Lord, hallelujah! Praise ye the Lord, hallelujah!
> Praise ye the Lord, hallelujah! Praise ye the Lord!

> *—Traditional; words of second line by Peter Young, 1995*

The Time of Remembering

Utilize a photo album that you have put together in advance showing the milestones in the life of the graduate. Open the album, and have one person select a photo and say, "I remember this . . ." Share the occasion with all present, and end with the words, "I thank God for such a meaningful time in the life of (*graduate's name*)." Repeat the process until everyone has had a chance to participate. Then have everyone sign the album, and present it to the graduate.

Another alternative is to use an autograph album. Have fellow graduates, teachers, friends, family, and others write some message to the graduate. Gather all of these messages prior to the home gathering celebration. During the time of remembering, take turns reading the various items that were written. It is a good opportunity for the graduate to realize the truly larger family to which she or he belongs. It would be appropriate to end this session by asking the graduate to lead you in prayer.

The Blessing

All place hands on graduate's head.

Parent: May the road rise to meet you.
　　　　　　May the wind be always at your back.
　　　　　　May the sun shine warm upon your face,
　　　　　　the rains fall soft upon your fields and,
　　　　　　until we meet again,
　　　　　　May God hold you in the palm of his hand.

All:　　　 Amen.

> *—Traditional Irish blessing*

For a kindergarten graduate, you may wish to use this blessing:

All: God goes with you

each step of the way.

God's love protects you

in all you do and say. Amen.

···Wedding Anniversary···

Most families have their own traditional ways of celebrating wedding anniversaries, so the following may be more appropriate for every fifth year or for the twenty-fifth- or fiftieth-year anniversaries. But it certainly could be used annually with meaning. You may wish to invite the pastor who married the couple and any other members of the wedding party who are in the area.

Begin the meal with the breaking of the bread only, and then after the meal, proceed to the lighting of the candles.

The Lighting of the Candles

Leader: Christ is the light of the world. Christ is the light of our lives.

The guests take turns lighting one candle for each year or each five years of marriage. As each candle is lit, you may wish to highlight one event during that time period by sharing a photograph of the occasion.

The Reading of the Word

After a meal:

All: As our bodies have been fed, O God, now feed our souls on your Word of life.

At other times:

All: May the light of your Word illumine our hearts.

The Spoken Response

All: Let your Word abide in us, O God.

The Special Celebration

One of the children, the pastor, or another guest should lead.

Wife: I am blessed to be your wife, and am happy in the love we have shared. I appreciate the deep commitment you have offered me, and the honest communication you have shared. I thank you for your compassion and understanding, your companionship, and your friendship. I rejoice in the joys and sorrows that have been ours, and the rich experiences we have known. May the years ahead be as richly blessed.

Husband: I am blessed to be your husband, and am happy in the love we have shared. I appreciate the deep commitment you have offered me, and the honest communication you have shared. I thank you for your compassion and understanding, your companionship, and your friendship. I rejoice in the joys and sorrows that have been ours, and the rich experiences we have known. May the years ahead be as richly blessed.

The Time of Remembering and Prayer

A prayer or a song such as "O Perfect Love" may be recited or sung at this time.

To celebrate this occasion, you may wish to start an anniversary scrapbook. Take a picture of everyone present. On each anniversary, as you light the candles, you may wish to reminisce about the times you have shared over the years, utilizing the scrapbook. Or you may prefer to make a quilt square to represent each anniversary. The item on the square could represent a significant event during the past year. Eventually, you may be able to make a pillow throw, a quilt, or maybe even two quilts—who knows!

The Extinguishing of the Candles

All: May the shalom, the peace of God, enfold us as the shadows of the night descend upon us. Amen.

Times of Significant Change

··· Moving to a New Community or a New Home ···

The time of moving is a time of ambivalence. We feel both hope and fear, both joy and sorrow. When the present home and community situations are positive and rewarding, family members often experience true grief when faced with leaving. They feel anger and denial. On the other hand, while the new home situation is as yet unknown, often the unknown itself is a challenge that opens up new possibilities for growth and joy. It is important to recognize these feelings of ambivalence and to celebrate them at this time of transition. Each family should determine the most appropriate time to celebrate, but it should be done before the entire household is physically disrupted in preparation for moving—maybe a week or so before the actual move is to take place.

The Song of Celebration
Sing a hymn expressing confidence in God's providence and love, such as "God of Our Life through All the Circling Years."

The Reading of the Word
After a meal:

All: As our bodies have been fed, O God, now feed our souls on your Word of life.

At other times:

All: May the light of your Word illumine our hearts.

A suggested passage of scripture is 1 Peter 1:1–9.

The Spoken Response

All: Let your Word abide in us, O God.

The Sung Response

Sing a hymn of your own choosing or use the following:

> Hallelu, hallelu, hallelu, hallelujah! Praise ye the Lord!
> For the light of your Word, and our gath'ring together, praise ye
>   the Lord!
> Praise ye the Lord, hallelujah! Praise ye the Lord, hallelujah!
> Praise ye the Lord, hallelujah! Praise ye the Lord!

—Traditional; words of second line by Peter Young, 1995

The Time of Remembering and Prayer

This is a time for the family to share the good memories of this home and community, to laugh and to weep together. A good way to involve all of the members of the family is to begin by saying, "I remember . . ." The time of remembering is very important for healing the wounds that may be incurred in moving. Take as much time as necessary. Conclude with a one-sentence prayer by each member of the family.

The Gathering and Blessing of the
Tokens of Remembrance

It is suggested that each person leave the gathering to collect one item that he or she wishes to give to another person, to leave behind as a symbol of continuity with the past and with past friends. Bring these back to the gathering.

Father: Gracious God, these gifts before us *(name each item)* represent an important part of our lives. They are a part of our past in this community. Bless them, we pray, that in the giving and in the receiving, they may bind us always to all that has been good and beautiful here. In the name of Christ, whose love binds all of us together.

All: Amen.

Family members now hold the gifts they have brought to the gathering.

All: God, our refuge always, our home is in you. May this place where we have lived and where we have found joys and sorrows be filled with blessings for those who follow us here. Protect us on our way, lead us to the love of new friends, lead us to a new community of faith, help us to be a home to one another through all of our lives, as you are our eternal home. Amen.

Blessing the Tokens of Remembrance (Alternative)

If the family is simply moving from one house in the community to another in the same or an adjacent community, invite your neighbors to a meal shortly before moving. Agree on some meaningful gift to give each family (for example, one of your plants that the family had admired). Use these in blessing the tokens of remembrance, and present them to the neighbors as the sharing.

Father: Gracious God, these gifts before us represent a part of our very lives. They are a part of our past in this neighborhood. Bless them, we pray, that in the giving and in the receiving, they may bind us always to all that has been good and beautiful here.

Present the gifts to each neighbor and have them hold them during the closing prayer.

Mother: God, our refuge always, our home is in you. May this place where we have lived and where we have found joys and sorrows be filled with blessing for those who follow us here. Protect us on our way, lead us to the love of new friends, but never let us forget old friends. Help us to be a home to one another through all of our lives, as you are our eternal home.

All: Amen.

The Extinguishing of the Candles

All: May the shalom, the peace of God, enfold us as we begin our preparations to follow where God has called us. Amen.

As soon as it is appropriate (possibly immediately following this celebration), family members should distribute the gifts to neighbors and friends.

At the time of moving, it is suggested that your home gathering centerpiece, which has served as the unifying focus for your family, be specially wrapped and carried with the family. This then can be one of the first things moved into the new home and be an immediate focus for both past and future.

···Arriving in a New Community or a New Home···

At the time of arrival in the new home, the home gathering centerpiece that you have brought with you should be carried into the new home and put in a position of prominence while the moving in takes place. As soon as possible, the family should hold a home gathering celebration in which this arrival ritual is used.

Before starting the home gathering, place an unlit candle in each room of the new home. Also purchase two small plants, two new pots, and some potting soil. Have these available for the celebration. Then gather at the place where you will keep the home gathering centerpiece, and perform the following celebration.

The Song of Celebration

Sing a hymn expressing thanksgiving for God's care and safekeeping in the course of the move—for example, "Now Thank We All Our God" or "Let Us with a Gladsome Mind." You may wish to use "God of Our Life, through All the Circling Years" to provide continuity with the moving celebration.

The Reading of the Word

All: As our bodies have been fed, O God, now feed our souls on your
           Word of life.

A good scripture might be Hebrews 11:1–12.

The Spoken Response

All: Let your Word abide in us, O God.

The Sung Response

Sing a hymn of your own choosing or use the following:

> Hallelu, hallelu, hallelu, hallelujah! Praise ye the Lord!
> For the light of your Word, and our gath'ring together, praise ye
>   the Lord!
> Praise ye the Lord, hallelujah! Praise ye the Lord, hallelujah!
> Praise ye the Lord, hallelujah! Praise ye the Lord!

—Traditional; words of second line by Peter Young, 1995

The Period of Prayer

If the family has moved from one home to another within the same or an adjacent community, change the words "new community" to "new neighborhood" in the prayer that follows.

Father: Abraham, heeding God's call, took his family and all that he owned, and walked by faith. The disciples, heeding Christ's call, left all that they had, and followed him by faith. We have come to this new home and new community (neighborhood) in response to God's call. We come by faith and in faith.

Mother: We place this candle (*or other symbol the family has been using*) in its accustomed place of honor in recognition that while we walk by faith, we walk not alone.

Light the Christ candle.

All: Christ is the light of the world. Christ is the light of our lives.

Father: Let us carry the light into all the rooms in our home, that Christ may truly be the light of this home for all who dwell here.

Next, all take turns lighting the candles throughout the house. As each candle is lit, they offer a brief prayer, such as "May this kitchen bring warmth and joy to our lives," or "May this bedroom bring peaceful rest." Then, they return to the worship center.

The Act of Transplanting and Blessing

*Members of the family should now transplant the two plants into the new pots.
Let one member of the family offer this blessing:*

Leader: Gracious God, you have caused the earth to put forth all kinds of plants. Some bear grain, some fruit. Others add to the beauty of our lives. Bless these plants which we have just transplanted. May they grow to add beauty to the lives of those around us. We also ask you to bless us as we have just been transplanted into this new community. May we grow to add beauty to the lives of those around us. In Christ's name we pray.

All: Amen.

As soon as it is appropriate, possibly right after this celebration, the family should go as a group to the neighbors on either side of their new home and present them with a plant of friendship.

The Extinguishing of the Candles

All: May the shalom, the peace of God, enfold us as we begin our new life where God has called us. Amen.

Home Blessing

Even if the family has merely moved from one home to another within the same or an adjacent community, you may wish to have your pastor use the ritual "New Home Blessing" on page 129. This home blessing ritual may also be used after you are completely moved into your new home. Instead of using it with a home gathering, you may wish to use it in conjunction with an open house for friends and neighbors, particularly from your larger family, the church.

···Changing Occupations···

Choosing one's occupation represents a time of significant change in one's life. It is also a time of uncertainty, and a time of challenge. Sometimes these changes are made by choice; sometimes the change comes about because of circumstances beyond one's control. In any case, the time of entering a new occupation or job is a time to celebrate. The following celebratory ritual is based on the call of Moses to a new occupation. Don't forget a "You Are Special" plate or your family equivalent.

The Song of Celebration
Let the person with the new position choose a favorite song or hymn to sing.

The Time of Challenge
You may use this in place of the usual reading of scripture.

Leader 1:   Moses was a happy man, a shepherd who daily watched his flocks. At night, he would return home to his family. He was content.

Leader 2:   The daily routine of his life and job provided him with a sense of safety and security. But read what happened to him.

The person with the new job reads Exodus 3:1–10.

Leader 1:   Change jobs! Go to Egypt! Speak to the king! Me! Moses was scared stiff! He said to God, "I am nobody. How can I go to the king?" Never!

Leader 2:   You see, Moses realized that a new job meant that he had to leave home, to leave his family and friends, to leave his safety and security.

Leader 1:   God understood how Moses felt. God assured Moses that in all circumstances God would be with him. Read about God's assurance.

The person with the new job reads Exodus 3:12–15.

Leader 2:   Moses still hesitated. He considered the future. Travel. Excitement. New experiences. Leadership. A chance to help others. A new job meant real challenge. And yet, he hesitated.

Leader 1:   It was then that God gave Moses a symbol. This symbol not only represented God's presence, but God's power that would sustain Moses wherever he was, whatever he faced.

The person with the new job reads Exodus 4:1–2.

Leader 2:   So tonight, we give you a symbol. May this symbol remind you not only of God's presence in your new venture, but also of our love and support.

Present the individual with an appropriate gift, such as a cross to hang on the wall in the new workplace or one to wear or carry in a pocket or purse. It may be something the family has made. As the symbol is presented, let each person offer the new employee a hug and kiss as a sign of love and support.

Leader 1:   May we, your loved ones, offer a word of caution and concern. Jobs today make a great many demands upon you. These are the demands of time, energy, loyalty, and conformity. We realize this, and we care.

Leader 2:   In your effort to do well, to succeed in your new job, to please your employer, you may forget your family, your friends, your other obligations, even your God. May these words that Moses heard be a constant reminder of your true calling and your God.

The person with the new job reads Exodus 20:1–17.

The Period of Prayer

Everyone joins hands and sings the words of the familiar hymn "Take My Life and Let It Be." Then each person offers a special prayer for the person with a new job.

The Blessing

Everyone places their hands on the head of the person with the new job.

All: God will bless you and take care of you. God will be kind and gracious to you. God will look on you with favor and give you peace. Amen.

The Extinguishing of the Candles

New employee: May the shalom, the peace of God, enfold us as the shadows of the night descend upon us.

All: Amen.

The Time of Celebration
Party! Enjoy the individual's favorite dessert. Offer congratulations! Talk about the changes and the challenges that lie ahead. Give gifts. Have fun!

··· Promotion or Special Honor ···

Promotion—at school, at work, in the service, in an organization—is a milestone that deserves a celebration. The same is true when a member of the family receives a special honor. It is a "You Are Special" plate occasion. Tailor your celebration to the age of the recipient and the type of promotion or honor. This is a time to invite friends to join in the celebration. Have fun!

The Song of Celebration
Use "Rise, Shine" from the regular home gathering celebration. It's a good praise song.

The Reading of the Word
Leader: On this special day, we ask (honoree's name) to read a special Word for us.

Honoree: It is good to give thanks to the Lord,
                  to sing praise to your name, O Most High;
                  to declare your steadfast love in the morning,
                  and your faithfulness by night,
                  to the music of the lute and the harp,
                  to the melody of the lyre.
                  For you, O Lord, have made me glad by your work;
                  at the works of your hands I sing for joy (Ps. 92:1–4).

The Sung Response
Have fun singing songs of joy and celebration. Use musical instruments; children may use rhythm instruments. Take as long as you want.

The Period of Prayer

We suggest that the honoree offer her or his own prayers at this time.

The Blessing

Everyone gathers around the honoree and places his or her hands on the honoree's head.

All: God has blessed you with this promotion/honor . Now we bless you with our love. Amen.

The Extinguishing of the Candles

Honoree: May the blessings of our gracious God enfold us all as we bring this celebration to a close.

All: Amen.

···Menopause or Climacteric ···

Menopause or climacteric (the male equivalent of menopause) represents a time of significant change in our lives, occurring around the ages of forty-five to fifty. In women, this time is marked by a physical change—the end of menstruation. No similar physical change is noted in men. For both, however, this period marks a time of transition which may be traumatic as well as liberating. This particular ritual is designed to help in dealing with the trauma, while leading to an affirmation of the life that lies ahead. It is a ritual that may need to be repeated several times during the period.

The Song of Celebration

Sing the first two verses of "Turn! Turn! Turn!"

TURN! TURN! TURN! (TO EVERYTHING THERE IS A SEASON)

Refrain: To ev'ry thing (*turn, turn, turn*)
There is a season (*turn, turn, turn*)
And a time for ev'ry purpose under heaven.

1. A time to be born, a time to die;
   A time to plant, a time to reap;
   A time to kill, a time to heal;
   A time to laugh, a time to weep. *(Refrain)*

2. A time to build up, a time to break down;
   A time to dance, a time to mourn;
   A time to cast away stones;
   A time to gather stones together. *(Refrain)*

3. A time of love, a time of hate;
   A time of war, a time of peace;
   A time you may embrace;
   A time to refrain from embracing. *(Refrain)*

4. A time to gain, a time to lose;
   A time to rend, a time to sew;
   A time to love, a time to hate;
   A time for peace, I swear it's not too late.

Words from the Book of Ecclesiastes, adapted and music by Pete Seeger.
TRO–©–Copyright 1962 (Renewed) Melody Trails, Inc.,
New York, NY. Used by permission.

The Reading of the Word and Time of Meditation

All: As our bodies have been fed, O God, now feed our souls on your Word of life.

Have an ashtray available in which you can burn small pieces of paper. Read Philippians 4:4–13 and take some time to meditate upon the words. Then read again the following texts and follow the instructions.

All: Do not worry about anything, but in everything by prayer and supplication with thanksgiving let your requests be made known to God (Phil. 4:6).

Write down the things that worry you, placing only one item on each slip of paper. With thanksgiving for this change in your life, offer these worries to God, one at a time, by burning them in the container. Since this change affects all members of the family, let everyone present participate.

All: Whatever is true, whatever is honorable, whatever is just, whatever is pure, whatever is pleasing, whatever is commendable, if
there is any excellence and if there is anything worthy of praise,
think about these things (Phil. 4:8).

*Write down the things that you see as freeing and liberating as this change takes
place. Write down your dreams for the future and, with thanksgiving, offer
them to God, one at a time, by burning them in the container. Again, all participate.*

All: I have learned to be content with whatever I have. . . . I can do
all things through the one who strengthens me (Phil. 4:11b, 13).

Pray in unison the Prayer of Our Savior.

The Song of Celebration
Sing verses 3 and 4 of "Turn! Turn! Turn!"

The Blessing and Extinguishing of Candles
All present place hands on head of the individual being honored.

All: May the shalom, the peace of God, rest upon you today and
always. Amen.

··· Retirement ···

In many ways, retirement is/can be a time of significant change similar to
menopause or climacteric, the male equivalent. It is a time of major transition that can be both traumatic and liberating. It should be an occasion for
which the individual has prepared a long time in advance, if it is to be truly
liberating. We suggest that the table be set with an additional home gathering
centerpiece using a small branch placed upright on a stand or in a flowerpot.
You may wish to spray the branch in silver or gold. Place a candle on either
side of the centerpiece. In front of one candle, place one or more symbols
representing the individual's occupation. In front of the other candle, place
one or more symbols representing the individual's hobbies. Have some paper,
pencils, and ribbon available for those present to use.

The Song of Celebration

Sing the first two verses of "Turn! Turn! Turn!" (see words on pages 43–44).

The Retirement Tree Ceremony

The retiree reads Ecclesiastes 3:1–13.

Leader: *(Retiree's name)*, this candle represents a very rich and significant part of your life. The jobs you have held have given meaning and purpose to the working hours of your days. They have helped you provide the means by which you and your family have been able to live. Please light this candle with joy and thanksgiving.

The retiree lights the candle and offers a prayer of thanksgiving.

Leader: Friends, family members, please take a piece of paper and write down one special memory you wish to share with *(retiree's name)* at this time. Also write down one special gift that you wish to give him/her. This can be a gift of yourself; it can be a special thing you will do with or for *(retiree's name)*; it may be the offer to buy a ticket to a special event; it can be whatever you would like.

   (Retiree's name), while your friends and family are doing this, you write down some of the special things you would like to do during your retirement. When you are all done, roll the paper up, tie it with a ribbon, and hang it on the retirement tree.

   Now, *(retiree's name)*, take the candle that represents the job from which you are retiring (or have retired), and light this second candle. This second candle represents the new life that lies ahead of you. Please light this candle with anticipation and thanksgiving, and then blow out the first candle.

The retiree lights a candle, offers a prayer of anticipation, and blows out the first candle.

Leader: Enjoy your retirement. When you feel the need, take one item from your retirement tree and celebrate life.

The Song of Celebration

Sing verses 3 and 4 of "Turn! Turn! Turn!" (see page 44).

The Blessing

Everyone present places his or her hands on the head of the retiree.

All: God will bless you and take care of you. God will be kind and gracious to you. God will look on you with favor and give you peace. Amen.

The Extinguishing of the Candles

Retiree: May the shalom, the peace of God, enfold us as the shadows of the night descend upon us.

All: Amen.

Times of **U**ncertainty

··· Before Entering the Hospital ···

Entering the hospital, even for same-day surgery, is usually a time of uncertainty and trauma. This is particularly so for children. It is suggested that you use this ritual on the evening before a family member enters the hospital.

The Song of Faith

Sing a verse or two of a familiar hymn of faith and trust such as "God's Eye Is on the Sparrow," "I've Got Peace like a River," or "O Love That Will Not Let Me Go." If the patient is a child, you may wish to sing "Jesus Loves Me."

The Reading of the Word

After a meal:

All: As our bodies have been fed, O God, now feed our souls on your Word of life.

At other times:

All: May the light of your Word illumine our hearts.

If possible, the person who is to be hospitalized should read his or her favorite Bible passage. Other suggested passages are Psalm 108:1–6; Psalm 42; or, for a child, Matthew 19:13–15.

The Spoken Response

All: Let your Word abide in us, O God.

The Sharing
Members of the family are encouraged to present some small token of love to the person who will enter the hospital. This might be a drawing made by a child to express love, "get well soon," or any other sentiment. It might be a small cross to remind them of the love and presence of God. The gifts should be small, personal, and meaningful.

The Period of Prayer
Join hands around the table. Let there be silence for as long as you feel appropriate. Let each member of the family who is able offer a prayer.

Leader: Gracious and loving God, you know the feelings of uncertainty and anxiety that *(person's name)* is going through, and that all of us have similar feelings. Help us to remember that you walk with us always, and especially in times of uncertainty. Even as you led the Hebrew people with a fire by night and a cloud of smoke by day to remind them of your presence, so lead us now by the light of the World. As *(person's name)* enters the hospital tomorrow, may s/he be aware of your presence and confident in your caring, healing love. We ask this in the name of Jesus, our Christ, who taught us to pray.

Pray in unison the Prayer of Our Savior.

The Blessing
All place their hands on head of person who will enter the hospital.

All: God will bless you and take care of you. God will be kind and gracious to you. God will look on you with favor and give you peace. Amen.

The Extinguishing of the Candles
All: May the shalom, the peace of God, enfold us and *(person's name)*, the one we love and care for so dearly. Amen.

··· While a Loved One Suffers or Is Dying ···

Dealing with the death of a loved one is difficult, but even more difficult is the sense of helplessness that comes when a loved one is suffering and/or is in the process of dying. We offer this little ritual that can be used every day to help see you through the seemingly endless waiting. This is a situation where memorization of psalms and hymns as a part of home and church training becomes a vital resource of the faith.

The Song of Faith

Sing a verse or two of a familiar hymn of faith and trust, such as "Abide with Me," or "How Sweet the Name of Jesus Sounds," or "He Leadeth Me, O Blessed Thought."

The Turning to the Word

Read—or better still, just repeat aloud—one of the more familiar psalms of faith and trust: 3, 23, 34, 42:1–5, 46, 89:1–4, 91, 113, 116, 121, 130, 136, or the shortest of all psalms, 117:

> Praise God, all you nations! Extol God, all you peoples! For great is God's steadfast love toward us, and the faithfulness of God . . . endures forever. Praise God!

If you are experiencing rage, anger, denial over the situation you face, try reading some of these psalms: 6, 13, 22, 25, 38, 77, 88, or 102—a portion of which follows:

> Hear my prayer, O God; let my cry come to you. Do not hide your face from me in the day of my distress. Incline your ear to me; answer me speedily in the day when I call. For my days pass away like smoke, and my bones burn like a furnace. My heart is stricken and withered like grass; I am too wasted to eat my bread. Because of my loud groaning my bones cling to my skin. I am like an owl of the wilderness, like an owl of the waste places. I lie awake; I am like a lonely bird on the housetop. All day long my enemies taunt me; those who deride me use my name for a

curse. For I eat ashes like bread, and mingle tears with my drink, because of your indignation and anger; for you have lifted me up and thrown me aside. My days are like an evening shadow; I wither away like grass. But you, O God, are enthroned forever; your name endures to all generations.

The Response

All: May the light of your Word give strength to our hearts.

The Period of Prayer

Enter into a prolonged period of quiet and wait for the awareness of the presence of God. Then let each person present offer whatever prayers may be in his or her heart. Conclude the prayer period with these words of Jesus:

All: If you are willing, remove this cup from me; yet, not my will but yours be done.

Pray in unison the Prayer of Our Savior.

The Blessing

In families with children present, use the following blessing.

Parents place their hands on the heads of the children.

Parents: May you love God, love yourself, and love your neighbor. May you walk always in the light of Jesus Christ.

Children hold hands with their parents.

Children: May our love for one another grow stronger day by day.

All: Amen.

If no children are present, everyone may say the blessing:

All: God bless you and take care of you. God be kind and gracious to you. God look on you with favor and give you peace. Amen.

The Extinguishing of the Candles

All: May the shalom, the peace of God, enfold us and (*person's name*), the one we love and care for so dearly. Amen.

··· Awaiting a Diagnosis ···

Very possibly, even more difficult than waiting while a loved one suffers is the uncertainty involved in waiting for a suspected illness or disability to be diagnosed in oneself or in a loved one. It is a time of high stress, a time when the stressors of life are not being managed. The key to dealing with such times rests in the shalom or serenity that comes from complete and abiding trust in our loving God.

The Song of Faith

Sing "Kum Ba Yah":

> Kum ba yah, my Lord, Kum ba yah!
>   Someone's crying, Lord, Kum ba yah . . .
> Kum ba yah, my Lord, Kum ba yah!
>   Someone's singing, Lord, Kum ba yah . . .
> Kum ba yah, my Lord, Kum ba yah!
>   Someone's praying, Lord, Kum ba yah . . .
> O Lord, Kum ba yah.
>   Someone's waiting, Lord, Kum ba yah . . .

> —*Traditional*

Add verses of your own. End with "Come by here, my Lord, come by here . . . "

The Reading of the Word

After a meal:

All: As our bodies have been fed, O God, now feed our souls and strengthen our hearts on your Word of life.

At other times:

All: Come to me, all you that are weary and are carrying heavy burdens, and I will give you rest (Matt. 11:28).

The Response

All: May the light of your Word give strength to our hearts.

The Period of Prayer

This is one time the family should definitely hold hands during the prayer period. Allow plenty of time for quiet. Then, one by one as the Spirit moves you, say: "I am weary. I give you my burden, my . . . " For example: "I give you my burden, my worries about the biopsy taken today," or "I give you my fear, my anxiety, my depression, my anger, my feelings of nervousness." When sufficient time has passed and you feel it is time to end the period of prayer, someone should start the Prayer of Our Savior, and all join in.

The Period of Conversation

This is a good time to talk about the various burdens you have placed in the hands of God. Talking things over often is the best way of chasing away the "demon" of uncertainty as well as one of the best ways of realizing that we do not face the difficulties and uncertainties of life alone.

The Blessing

Place hands on head of person awaiting diagnosis.

All: God will bless you and take care of you. God will be kind and gracious to you. God will look on you with favor and give you peace. Amen.

The Extinguishing of the Candles

All: May we completely trust the shalom, the serenity, the peace of God, as the darkness of night descends upon us. Amen.

··· In the Face of Illness or Serious Accident ···

Illness and accidents happen; they are simply a part of life. But they always disrupt the routine and add a burden of stress to our lives. Using your regular home gathering celebration with some of the following suggestions should help place the illness or accident in proper perspective. It should also provide you with an additional tool for dealing with these stressors. If the person who is ill or injured is at home but not able to come to the table, have the home gathering in his or her room.

The Song of Celebration

This may be another occasion when you use "Turn! Turn! Turn!" (see pages 43–44) or the familiar hymn "Be Still, My Soul."

The Reading of the Word

After a meal:

All: As our bodies have been fed, O God, now feed our souls on your Word of life.

At other times:

All: May the light of your Word illumine our hearts.

Select a passage that affirms God's love, such as the following passage from the eighth chapter of the book of Romans:

> We know that all things work together for good for those who love God. . . . What then are we to say about these things? If God is for us, who is against us? . . . Who will separate us from the love of Christ? Will hardship, or distress, or persecution, or famine, or nakedness, or peril, or sword? . . . No, in all these things we are more than conquerors through him who loved us. For I am convinced that neither death, nor life, nor angels, nor rulers, nor things present, nor things to come, nor powers, nor height, nor depth, nor anything else in all creation, will be able to separate us from the love of God in Christ Jesus. (Rom. 8:28, 31, 35, 37, 38, 39)

The Response

All: Let your Word abide in us, O God.

The Period of Prayer

If the person who is ill or injured is present, all others gather around and place their hands gently on him or her.

All: Come, Holy Spirit, come.

Come with love, and offer assurance.

Come with power, and bring healing.

Come with shalom, and grant serenity.

Pray in unison the Prayer of Our Savior.

The Blessing

With hands still on the individual's head pray:

All: God will bless you and take care of you. God will be kind and gracious to you. God will look on you with favor and give you peace. Amen.

The Extinguishing of the Candles

All: May we completely trust that the shalom, the serenity, the peace of God, will rest upon *(injured person's name)*, the one we love and care for so dearly. Amen.

Times of Significant Loss

···Death···

We have learned that most people go through a variety of reactions to any type of significant loss. Deep-seated responses follow the loss of a job, the loss of a limb, the loss of a loved one through death, and even the loss of an emotional or physiological crutch such as alcohol. The rituals that follow are designed around the traditionally designated reactions: denial, anger, bargaining, depression, and acceptance. We begin with death and suggest that this celebration be held as soon as possible following the funeral. In addition to the Christ candle, we suggest that one candle be lit for each person present and one for the deceased.

The Lighting of the Candles
All: Christ is the light of the world. Christ is the light of our lives. But the light is dimmed by our tears.

The Song of Celebration
Sing any Easter hymn or a favorite hymn of the deceased.

The Readings from the Word
All: As our bodies have been fed, O God, now feed our souls on your Word of life.

Take turns reading the following passages or others of your choice:

> It is useless, useless, said the Philosopher. Life is useless, all useless. You spend your life working, laboring, and what do you have to show for it? Generations come and generations go, but the world stays just the same.

56

The sun still rises, and it still goes down, going wearily back to where it must start all over again. The wind blows south, the wind blows north—round and round and back again. Every river flows to the sea, but the sea is not yet full. The water returns to where the river began, and starts all over again. Everything leads to weariness—a weariness too great for words (Eccles. 1:2–8a TEV).

My God, my God, why have you forsaken me? Why are you so far from helping me, from the words of my groaning? O my God, I cry by day, but you do not answer; and by night, but find no rest. . . . Yet it was you who took me from the womb; you kept me safe on my mother's breast. On you I was cast from my birth, and since my mother bore me you have been my God. Do not be far from me, for trouble is near and there is no one to help. . . . O Lord, do not be far away! O my help, come quickly to my aid! (Ps. 22:1–2, 9–11, 19)

Jesus said to her, "I am the resurrection and the life. Those who believe in me, even though they die, will live; and everyone who lives and believes in me will never die." (John 11:25, 26a)

Peace I leave with you; my peace I give you. I do not give to you as the world gives. Do not let your hearts be troubled, and do not let them be afraid. (John 14:27)

The Response
All: Let your Word abide in us, O God.

The Time of Sharing
Let each person hold up his or her candle and share a good memory of the deceased. Go around the table as many times as you feel necessary, saying, "I remember . . ."

The Period of Prayer
Enter into a period of quiet and then have someone offer the following:
Leader: O God, we find it so hard to believe that *(deceased's name)* has
                     died. We loved him/her so very much, and our hearts are broken.

Sometimes we turn around to share a thought with him/her, but (*deceased's name*) is not there. We do not want to believe, we cannot believe that s/he will never return.

The pain of his/her absence is great. We cry out with the pain. We cry out with anger both at the unfairness of his/her leaving us behind, and at the unfairness of you doing this to us. But even in our anger, we realize that you truly are good, that life is good, that death is good, because life and death are a part of the larger plan of life you have for us all.

There is real sadness in our hearts. We are not really sure that we can face tomorrow and all the tomorrows that will come without (*deceased's name*). We are not sure that we want to. And yet, we are reminded of those beautiful words of the psalmist, "Weeping may linger for the night, but joy comes with the morning" (Ps. 30:5).

Let us not stay in the depths of our despair, but lift us up! Grant us strength for the tasks that lie ahead! Set before us a renewed sense of your vision for our lives! May the presence of our risen Christ enable us to place our full faith and confidence in you, gracious God.

Thank you for the life we have been privileged to share. Thank you for receiving our beloved to yourself in eternal life. Thank you for life and for death.

Pray in unison the Prayer of Our Savior.

The Extinguishing of the Candles

Extinguish all but the one set aside for the departed. Allow that one to burn for the rest of the evening.

All: May the shalom, the peace of God, enfold us as the darkness of our grief descends upon us. Amen.

··· Sudden Infant Death (SIDS) or Death of a Young Child ···

In addition to the feelings of denial, anger, bargaining, depression, and (one hopes) acceptance, the sudden death of an infant or the death of a young child also brings out tremendous feelings of guilt, self-condemnation, and other feelings of pain so deep as to defy categorization. It is vital that there be some type of church gathering to express the loving, caring, supporting community of faith. But it is also important to have a home gathering that is special, and then to include a special act of remembrance in each home gathering thereafter, for as long a time as the family deems necessary.

The Lighting of the Candles

The father lights the Christ candle. The mother lights the candle of remembrance.

All: Christ is the light of the world. Christ is the light of our lives. Christ, come shine on this sorrowing family.

The Lighting of the Candles in Future Home Gatherings

The father lights the Christ candle.

Father: Christ is the light of the world. Christ is the light of our lives.

The mother lights the remembrance candle.

Mother: Christ is the light of *(child's name).*

The Blessing

If no meal is served, omit this blessing.

All: In praise of you, O God, we break this bread *(break a piece of bread)*, for by your gracious love we all are nourished and sustained. Amen.

Share the bread.

The Song of Faith

Sing, for there is healing in song. Use this adaptation of the traditional spiritual "There Is a Balm in Gilead" or any other with which you feel comfortable:

There is a balm in Gilead to make the wounded whole;

There is a balm in Gilead to heal the broken soul.

Sometimes I feel discouraged, and think my life's in vain,

But then the Holy Spirit revives my soul again.

—Traditional. Adaptation by Peter Young, 1994

The Reading of the Word

All: As our bodies have been fed, O God, now feed our souls on your Word of life.

You may use any of the suggested scriptures from the previous ritual, or you may wish to use Mark 10:13–16 and Psalm 23. Conclude with the following:

> Why are you cast down, O my soul, and why are you disquieted within me? Hope in God; for I shall again praise God, my help and my God. (Ps. 42:11)

The Time of Sharing

It is important to express the depth of your feelings. Sharing your loss, your grief, brings healing. It would be appropriate to hold up something that belonged to your child and talk about your dreams for your future life together. Let your tears flow, for these, too, are appropriate. Many people find expression of their feelings by writing poetry, a song, or even a letter to the child. Take whatever time you need, and close with a time of silence as you lead into the prayer period.

The Period of Prayer

All: Words cannot express the depth of our feelings, O God. The bitterness and the pain, the sense of loss and grief, the anger and frustration, the guilt and sense of our own failure—all are too much for us. Please make us aware of your loving presence. Please ease our pain. Please heal our hearts.

We would pray the prayer of (*child's name*), saying: Now I lay me down to sleep, I pray thee, Lord, my soul to keep. If I should die before I wake, I pray thee, Lord, my soul to take. Amen.

Pray in unison the Prayer of Our Savior.

The Blessing

In families where there are other children, it is important to continue to use the traditional home gathering blessing.

Parents place their hands on the heads of the children.

Parents: May you love God, love yourself, and love your neighbor.
          May you walk always in the light of Jesus Christ.

Children hold hands with their parents.

Children: May our love for one another grow stronger day by day.

All: Amen.

If no children are present, everyone may say the blessing:

All: God bless you and take care of you. God be kind and gracious to
          you. God look on you with favor and give you peace. Amen.

The Extinguishing of the Candles

Extinguish the Christ candle, but allow the remembrance candle to burn for the remainder of the evening.

All: May the shalom, the peace of God, enfold us as the depth of our
          grief descends upon us. Amen.

··· Miscarriage or Stillborn Child ···

Most of what was said in the introductory remarks to the ritual on sudden infant death and most of the material suggested for that ritual are appropriate at this particular time of significant loss. We offer some additional materials focusing on both the loss of the child's life potential and the need to accept the difficult situation.

The Lighting of the Candles

The father should light the Christ candle. The mother should light the candle of remembrance.

All: Christ is the light of the world. Christ is the light of our lives.
          Christ, come shine on this sorrowing family.

The Lighting of the Candles in Future Home Gatherings

The father lights the Christ candle.

Father: Christ is the light of the world. Christ is the light of our lives.

The mother lights the remembrance candle.

Mother: Christ is the light of *(child's name)*.

The Song of Faith

Sing, for there is healing in song. Use this adaptation of the traditional spiritual "There Is a Balm in Gilead" or any other with which you feel comfortable:

> There is a balm in Gilead to make the wounded whole;
>
> There is a balm in Gilead to heal the broken soul.
>
> Sometimes I feel discouraged, and think my life's in vain,
>
> But then the Holy Spirit revives my soul again.

—Traditional; adaptation by Peter Young, 1994

The Reading of the Word

Mother: As our bodies have been fed, O God,

Father: Now feed our souls on your Word of life.

Mother: Hear my prayer, O God; let my cry come to you.

Father: Do not hide your face from me in the day of my distress.

Both: Incline your ear to me; answer me speedily in the day when I call! (Ps. 102:1–2).

The mother reads Psalm 77:1–12; the father reads Psalm 46.

Both: Why are you cast down, O my soul, and why are you disquieted within me? Hope in God; for I shall again praise this one, my help and my God (Ps. 42:11).

The Sharing

It is important to express the depth of your feelings. Sharing your loss, your grief, brings healing. It would be appropriate to hold up some item you have already purchased for your child and talk about your dreams for your future life together. Let your tears flow, for these, too, are appropriate. Many people find expression of their feelings by writing poetry, a song, or even a letter to the child. Take as much time as you need.

The Period of Prayer

Begin with a prolonged period of silence. Then in confidence and trust, pray:

All: God grant us the serenity to accept the things we cannot
        change . . .

        particularly the death of this child, whose life and love we will
        never share . . .

        the courage to change the things we can . . .

        our feelings of anger and guilt, our pain, our emptiness . . .

        and the wisdom to know the difference . . .

        by full and complete trust in your love and grace. Amen.

—Reinhold Niebuhr, adapted by Peter Young

Pray in unison the Prayer of Our Savior.

The Blessing

In families where there are other children, it is important to continue to use
the traditional home gathering blessing.

Parents place their hands on the heads of the children.

Parents: May you love God, love yourself, and love your neighbor. May
        you walk always in the light of Jesus Christ.

Children hold hands with their parents.

Children: May our love for one another grow stronger day by day.

All: Amen.

If no children are present, everyone may say the blessing:

All: God bless you and take care of you. God be kind and gracious to
        you. God look on you with favor and give you peace. Amen.

The Extinguishing of the Candles

*Extinguish the Christ candle, but allow the remembrance candle to burn for
the remainder of the evening.*

All: May the shalom, the peace of God, enfold us as the depth of our
        grief descends upon us. Amen.

··· The Loss of Part of One's Life ···

Death isn't the only time of significant loss in our lives. Often the loss of a significant part of one's life is as traumatic as death itself. The loss of a limb, the loss of a job, the loss of a family farm, the loss of a home by fire, the loss of a beloved family pet, even the loss of the false emotional support gained temporarily through alcohol, caffeine, nicotine, or other drugs can be as painful and grief-producing as death. To utilize a special home gathering ritual at these times of loss will help provide breathing space needed to enable us to reestablish order and tranquillity in our lives.

The Lighting of the Candles
All: Christ is the light of the world. Christ is the light of our lives. But the light is dimmed by our tears.

The Song of Faith
Sing "Kum Ba Yah":

> Kum ba yah, my Lord, Kum ba yah!
>   Someone's crying, Lord, Kum ba yah . . .
> Kum ba yah, my Lord, Kum ba yah!
>   Someone's singing, Lord, Kum ba yah . . .
> Kum ba yah, my Lord, Kum ba yah!
> Someone's praying, Lord, Kum ba yah . . .
>   O Lord, Kum ba yah.
> Someone's waiting, Lord, Kum ba yah . . .

> *—Traditional*

Add verses of your own. End with the following line, and hum softly as you lead into the reading of the Word:

> Come by here, my Lord, come by here . . .

The Reading of the Word

The person who has suffered the loss or a family member leads. If it is a loss that affects the entire family, any member may serve as the leader.

Leader: It is at a time like this that I know just how Job felt when he cried out:

> Why is light given to one in misery, and life to the bitter in soul, who long for death, but it does not come, and dig for it more than for hidden treasures; who rejoice exceedingly, and are glad when they find the grave? Why is light given to one who cannot see the way, whom God has fenced in? For my sighing comes before my bread, and my groanings are poured out like water. Truly the thing that I fear comes upon me, and what I dread befalls me. I am not at ease, nor am I quiet; I have no rest; but trouble comes. (Job 3:20–26)

Leader: It is at a time like this that I know just how the psalmist felt when he said:

> Incline your ear, O God, and answer me, for I am poor and needy. . . . You are my God; be gracious to me, . . . for to you do I cry all day long. . . . Give ear, O God, to my prayer; listen to my cry of supplication.

Leader: But I also am able to affirm with the psalmist:

> In the day of my trouble I call on you, for you will answer me. There is none like you among the gods, O God, nor are there any works like yours. . . . I give thanks to you, O . . . my God, with my whole heart, and I will glorify your name forever. For great is your steadfast love toward me; you have delivered my soul from the depths of Sheol. (Ps. 86:1, 3, 6–8, 12–13)

The Response

All: May the light of your Word give comfort and strength to our souls. Amen.

The Period of Prayer and Symbolic Committal

Have available a small box, a piece of paper, a pen, and something symbolic of the loss, such as a pet's collar, a small piece of wood from a home destroyed by fire or flood, and so on.

Family member: *(Person's name)*, we share in your grief. We would also share in this time of burying your loss and moving on in faith. Please write down your loss and a brief description of the pain you feel, then place the paper in the box along with a symbol of your loss.

Leader: Let us pray together.

All: O God, gracious and merciful, we acknowledge that you are the source of all life, of all that we have and are. We know that you, too, have felt the grief and pain of loss, even of your beloved Child. Yet it was through your Child that you told us to place our burdens in your care. Today we share the pain of *(person's name)* and the loss of his/her *(name loss)*. By this act of burial, we entrust that loss to your special care and keeping. We pray that the knowledge that this loss is now in your good hands will bring healing and peace to the one we love.

Leader: In the name of Christ, who taught us to pray.

Pray in unison the Prayer of Our Savior.

The Blessing

Parents place their hands on the heads of the children.

Parents: May you love God, love yourself, and love your neighbor. May you walk always in the light of Jesus Christ.

Children hold hands with their parents.

Children: May our love for one another grow stronger day by day.

All: Amen.

If no children are present, everyone may say the blessing:

All: God bless you and take care of you. God be kind and gracious to you. God look on you with favor and give you peace. Amen.

The Extinguishing of the Candles

Leader: May the shalom, the peace of God, enfold us as the depth of our grief descends upon us.

All: Amen.

At the close of the home gathering, everyone should adjourn to the yard or other appropriate place, if possible. Select a place to bury the box, and do so. Let the grieving person(s) do the actual burying, and conclude by saying:

Bereaved person: Into your hands I/we commend my/our loss.

··· Divorce, Separation, or Broken Engagement ···

A broken engagement, a formal or informal separation in a marriage, and divorce all indicate a significant loss in one's life. This is a time of disappointment, self-contempt, guilt, anger, frustration, feelings of failure, and pain. It is a time when individuals go through much the same grieving process as with death itself. It is a time of brokenness that cries out for healing. It is real and needs holding up to the light of the Light of Lights. A "broken" wooden cross, one that can be taken apart and put back together again, could be used in this ritual in place of the usual home gathering symbol. Have it taken apart for the ritual.

The Lighting of the Candles
All: Christ is the light of the world. Christ is the light of our lives. But the light is dimmed by our tears.

The Song of Faith
You may wish to sing "There Is a Balm in Gilead," "Kum Ba Yah," or one of your own favorite hymns.

The Reading of the Word
Leader: In our brokenness we turn to the living Word for healing and wholeness. May the light of God's Word illumine our hearts and brighten our lives.

Suggested passages of scripture are Psalm 57, Psalm 63, Psalm 86, Ezekiel 37:1–14, John 14:27, Romans 8:31–39. Conclude with these words of hope from Isaiah:

> Thus says God, "Do not remember the former things, or consider the things of old. I am about to do a new thing; now it springs forth, do you not perceive it?" (Isa. 43:18, 19a).

The Response

All: May the light of your Word bring comfort to our hearts.

The Symbolic Act of Healing

You will need some item that represents the wholeness of the relationship that was broken. For example, an engagement ring, a marriage certificate, or the like. All stand in a circle around the individual whose relationship has been broken, who will hold up the item representing the relationship. That person leads.

Leader: This *(name item)* represents a relationship of love that once was beautiful and whole. I will remember and cherish the good, but now would put the hurt and sadness of the relationship behind me.

The leader places the item behind his or her back, and a member of the circle takes it away.

Leader: I now take this cross, symbolic of the brokenness of a relationship I once found beautiful and good. I put the cross back together, remembering that it was through the cross of Jesus Christ that God restored the ultimate broken relationship.

The leader puts the cross back together again.

Leader: Gracious God, I realize that there were many good things in the relationship now broken that should be remembered and cherished, and I truly give you thanks for them. I realize that it was a love born of your spirit that brought us together in the first place. But I have now come to a time of separation, a time of pain, a time of brokenness, and I pray that you will help both of us not to "cling to the events of the past or dwell on what happened long ago" (Isa. 43:18 TEV). Rather, by the strength of your spirit, enable us to forgive, to forget, and to move into a new day. Release us from vows we can no longer keep. Heal our wounds.

All: Grant your peace. In the name of the Jesus, who brought us peace. Amen.

The Extinguishing of the Candles

All: Christ is the light of the world. Christ is the light of our lives. The light that was dimmed by our tears now shines brighter.

The Extinguishing of the Candles (Alternative)

All: May the shalom, the peace of God, enfold us as the shadows of night descend upon us. Amen.

A little booklet, *Life after Divorce*, compiled by Dorothy Payne and published by The Pilgrim Press, is very helpful even at the time of a broken engagement or separation. We share with you a portion of the introduction and one of the prayers written by Ms. Payne:

> For a short time after I was divorced, I looked around for someone to fill the void. It was a mad search that rose from my loneliness, guilt, and fear. It was not satisfying. It made me feel more fearful, guilty, and desperate. I thought that if I didn't have someone near me I would have too much space to think. I didn't want to think for fear of what I'd discover.
>
> At last I decided to face the dark shadows in my own mind and heart. As I grew in myself I had less and less need for the approval of others. As I turned to God and within myself for strength and comfort I realized that I was being my own worst condemner. I was much harder on myself, demanded more of myself, than anyone else would have thought of doing. . . .
>
> God does not expect us to be more than we were created to be. None of us has to be a wonderful, joyous, strong, loving person immediately. If we love God, those qualities will come. This is a reality full of hope. . . .

Dear God of my future and my hope, I know you are calling me forward and I'm learning slowly to trust your great compassion and forgiveness. I do not know where I am going, but I do know I want to do what is pleasing in your sight, go where you want me to go. I know that if I listen to my own heart you will lead me by the right road though I may be surprised when I find myself on it. I know I need not fear because you will never leave me alone. I praise you for blessing me so richly. Keep me faithful, God, now and forevermore. Amen.[9]

Times of Separation

··· First Separations ···

First separations are times of both joy and trauma. They are times of joy because they are signs of growth and maturing. They are times of trauma because they are just that, separations. We suggest that this little ceremony, with appropriate modifications to meet your specific family situation, might be used on the occasion of a child's first day of school, a first overnight visit alone, the first time he or she attends camp, etc. This is a "You Are Special" plate occasion. During a regular home gathering on the evening before the separation, allow the child to light the candle and extinguish it.

The Song of Celebration
Use a favorite song of the child involved.

The Reading of the Word
After a meal:

All: As our bodies have been fed, O God, now feed our souls on your Word of life.

At other times:

All: May the light of your Word illumine our hearts.

If the child has a favorite passage of scripture, read it; or you may wish to read Matthew 28:16–20, 1 Samuel 20:41–42, or Ecclesiastes 3:1–8.

The Spoken Response
All: Let your Word abide in us, O God.

The Sung Response

Sing a hymn of your own choosing or use the following:

Hallelu, hallelu, hallelu, hallelujah! Praise ye the Lord!
For the light of your Word, and our gath'ring together, praise ye
the Lord!
Praise ye the Lord, hallelujah! Praise ye the Lord, hallelujah!
Praise ye the Lord, hallelujah! Praise ye the Lord!

—Traditional; words of second line by Peter Young, 1995

The Sharing

This is a good time to give the child some item to serve as a reminder that you and God will be with her or him even in the separation. For example, if the child is going to camp, the gift of a compass would symbolize the desire that the child always be able to find the way home.

The Period of Prayer

Mother: Our Bible tells us that "everything that happens in this world happens at the times God chooses. . . . God sets the times for sorrow and the times for joy" (Eccles. 3:1, 4a TEV). God also sets the times for separation and the times for reunion. Today (or tomorrow) is one of those times God has set for separation.

Father: It is a time of both sorrow and joy. We will all be sorry to be separated from you. We will miss your being with us. But we will all be happy that this is a day of growing up for you.

Each family member: I love you. I will miss you, but I will be with you in your heart.

Mother: God will be with you, too.

Father: Because God loves you.

Child: Thank you. I will be sad, but I will be happy, too. I know that I will not be alone. When I return, I will share my joy with you.

All present join hands around the table. Each person offers a special prayer for the child. The child concludes by leading the family in the prayer Jesus taught his disciples.

The Blessing

Parents place their hands on the heads of the children.

Parents: May you love God, love yourself, and love your neighbor. May you walk always in the light of Jesus Christ.

Children hold hands with their parents.

Children: May our love for one another grow stronger day by day.

All: Amen.

The Extinguishing of the Candles

Allow the child who is going away to lead.

Leader: May the shalom, the peace of God, enfold us and be with us in our separation, even as the shadows of night now descend upon us.

All: Amen.

···Leaving Home···

First separations are not the only times of both joy and trauma—all separations are. They are signs of joy because they usually mark a new, exciting phase of living. They are times of trauma because they are times of breaking apart. You may find the following celebratory ritual of value when a young person leaves home to live independently, to attend college, to get married, or to enter military service. This is a "You Are Special" plate occasion. Have the person who is leaving light and extinguish the candles for the home gathering.

The Song of Celebration

Sing "Turn! Turn! Turn!" (see pages 43–44) or "Lonesome Valley," or enjoy yourself with the familiar children's song "Down in My Heart,"[10] which begins, "I have the joy, joy, joy, joy, down in my heart." Add your own words to suit the occasion.

The Reading of the Word

After a meal:

All: As our bodies have been fed, O God, now feed our souls on your Word of life.

At other times:

All: May the light of your Word illumine our hearts.

Scriptures suggested for different occasions include:

> Independent living: All or part of Proverbs 8.
> College: All or part of Proverbs 4.
> Marriage: Genesis 2:21–24.
> Military service: Romans 8:31–39.

The Spoken Response

All: Let your Word abide in us, O God.

The Sung Response

Sing a hymn of your own choosing or use the following:

> Hallelu, hallelu, hallelu, hallelujah! Praise ye the Lord!
> For the light of your Word, and our gath'ring together, praise ye
>   the Lord!
> Praise ye the Lord, hallelujah! Praise ye the Lord, hallelujah!
> Praise ye the Lord, hallelujah! Praise ye the Lord!

> *—Traditional; words of second line by Peter Young, 1995*

The Sharing

This is an appropriate time to give a gift of remembrance to the person leaving. If there are younger children in the family, they can make something special.

The Period of Prayer

Each person present shares a good experience from the past.

All: Thanks be to God.

Each person present offers a special prayer for the future.

All: Hear our prayer, O God.

The Blessing

All present gather around the special person and place their hands on his or her head.

All: God will bless our love for one another. God will bless you and take care of you. God will be kind and gracious to you. God will look on you with favor now and always. Amen.

The Extinguishing of the Candles

Person leaving: May the shalom, the peace of God, enfold us, together and separated, as the shadows of the night descend upon us.

All: Amen.

···Placing a Loved One in a Nursing Home···

This is one of the most difficult times of separation. It is important that three particular aspects of this time be faced honestly and dealt with honestly: (1) the fear that entering a nursing home will mean the loss of contact with one's family, (2) the concern that this is the end of the individual's usefulness and meaning, and (3) the usually unexpressed feeling that this is just a way of marking time until one dies. In addition, the family member or members who remain outside the nursing home have to recognize that they will be going through a true grieving process, along with the person entering the home, and that there may be enormous feelings of guilt. To help deal with these concerns, we suggest the following materials, particularly the prayer litany based on Psalm 42 TEV.

The Song of Celebration

Sing "Lord of All Hopefulness" or some other appropriate hymn.

The Reading of the Word

After a meal:

All: As our bodies have been fed, O God, now feed our souls on your Word of life.

At other times:

All: May the light of your Word illumine our hearts.

A suggested scripture is Romans 8:31–39.

The Spoken Response

All: Let your Word abide in our hearts, giving us love and under-
              standing.

The Sung Response

Sing a hymn of your own choosing or use the following:

> Hallelu, hallelu, hallelu, hallelujah! Praise ye the Lord!
> For the light of your Word, and our gath'ring together, praise ye
>   the Lord!
> Praise ye the Lord, hallelujah! Praise ye the Lord, hallelujah!
> Praise ye the Lord, hallelujah! Praise ye the Lord!

—Traditional; words of second line by Peter Young, 1995

The Sharing

It is suggested that the individual who is entering the nursing home be asked
to decide on a special concern to receive the mealtime offering. Place a special box with the home gathering centerpiece to indicate this concern. Thus,
whenever anything is placed in the box, the family member will be honored
and remembered.

The Period of Prayer

Leader: As a deer longs for a stream of cool water, so we long for you, O
              God. We thirst for you, our living God, in the midst of the pain
              of separation. Day and night we cry, and tears are our only food.

Share the concerns of the separation—that which each person will cry about.

All: Why are we so sad? Why are we so troubled? We will put our
              hope in God and once again will praise God's holy name.

Leader: Our hearts break when we remember the past, when we went
              with the crowds to the house of God and led them as they walked
              along, a happy crowd, singing and shouting praise to God.

Share the happy times that you remember and will continue to remember.

All: Why are we so sad? Why are we so troubled? We will put our
              hope in God and once again will praise God's holy name.

Leader: Here in exile our hearts are breaking, and so we turn our thoughts to God. We feel that God has sent waves of sorrow over our souls; chaos roars at us like a flood, like waterfalls thundering down to the Jordan from Mount Hermon. We feel angry. We feel lost. We feel alone. We feel pressed down into the depths.

Share the anger, the hurt, the pain.

All: Why are we so sad? Why are we so troubled? We will put our hope in God and once again will praise God's holy name.

Leader: May God show us constant love during each day, that we may feel worthwhile and useful, that we may have a song in our hearts at night. This we pray to the God of our lives.

Share a commitment to maintain contact and ways of enabling the individual to still feel a part of the family and useful to others.

All: Why are we so sad? Why are we so troubled? We will put our hope in God and once again will praise God's holy name.

Pray in unison the Prayer of Our Savior.

The Blessing

All present hold the person who is entering the nursing home.

All: God will bless our love for one another. God will bless you and take care of you. God will be kind and gracious to you. God will look on you with favor and give you peace. Amen.

The Extinguishing of the Candles

The person entering the nursing home should be given the privilege of extinguishing the candle and leading.

Leader: May the shalom, the peace of God, enfold us as the shadows of the night descend upon us.

All: Amen.

···Returning···

You may wish to celebrate the return of any individual for whom you have held a leaving-home ritual. This is usually a particularly joyful occasion, and everyone should be in a particularly festive mood. Special decorations may be in order. Certainly the individual's favorite foods and desserts are in order. This is a true "You Are Special" plate occasion.

If a son or daughter is returning home because of a marital separation or divorce, we suggest that you refer to the section on divorce, separation, or broken engagement beginning on page 67.

The Songs of Celebration

Sing, sing, and sing some more. Sing the returnee's favorites. Sing the family favorites. Sing camp songs. Sing fun songs. Sing hymns. Why not start off with the following:

> Let us sing together; Let us sing together; One and all a joyous song.
> Let us sing together; One and all a joyous song.
> Let us sing again and again, Let us sing again and again,
> Let us sing again and again, One and all a joyous song.

—Traditional

The Reading of the Word

After a meal:

All: As our bodies have been fed, O God, now feed our souls on your Word of life.

At other times:

All: May the light of your Word illumine our hearts.

Have the returnee read all or part of Psalm 145.

The Spoken Response

All: Let your Word abide in us, O God.

The Sung Response

Sing a hymn of your own choosing or use the following:

Hallelu, hallelu, hallelu, hallelujah! Praise ye the Lord!

For the light of your Word, and our gath'ring together, praise ye the
Lord!

Praise ye the Lord, hallelujah! Praise ye the Lord, hallelujah!

Praise ye the Lord, hallelujah! Praise ye the Lord!

—Traditional; words of second line by Peter Young, 1995

The Sharing

Let this be a fun time of talking about the individual's experiences. Give the
returnee plenty of time to talk, to share pictures, souvenirs, and the like.

The Period of Prayer

Let there be prayers of joy and thanksgiving from everyone present. You may
wish to conclude with this prayer:

Leader: O God, you are so good, your love and your mercy are everlasting.
We thank you so much for the safe return home of our beloved
(person's name). The time of separation has been difficult for all
of us, and yet it has also been a time of joy for all of us. We thank
you for keeping us bound together through the ties of love and
your spirit. We thank you for the wonderful opportunity that
(person's name) had. May it be for him/her a constant reminder
of the wonders of your creation and the joys of your life. May the
knowledge gained, the relationships formed, and the experiences
shared serve *(person's name)* throughout life. Thank you for
watching over her/him. Thank you for watching over all of us.
Thank you, in the name and spirit of Jesus our Christ.

All: Amen.

The Blessing and Extinguishing of the Candle

Returnee: God will bless our love for one another. God will bless you and
take care of you. God will be kind and gracious to you. God will
look on you with favor as the shalom, the peace of God, enfolds
us this night.

All: Amen.

Times of Special Concern

···The Overwhelming Sense of Sin/Brokenness and Reconciliation···

A celebration at a time when a member of the family is attempting to deal with an overwhelming sense of sin or brokenness may not seem to be very appropriate, particularly in the home gathering setting of a meal. It is our contention, however, that such a setting may be the most appropriate setting for dealing with sin, brokenness, and reconciliation. The sacramental act of penance and absolution in the Roman Catholic tradition may be helpful in conveying forgiveness when the sense of brokenness is between the individual and God. The confessional act and assurance of pardon in the corporate worship of the Protestant tradition may be helpful in conveying forgiveness in general. But neither approach brings together the specific sin/brokenness and the corporate caring, interceding, forgiving that can occur in the home. The closest our society experiences this is in the context of Alcoholics Anonymous, other twelve-step programs, and similar types of gatherings—usually lacking a specific Christian context.

It is desirable to have present at the gathering the individual or individuals from whom the family member feels alienated. It may also be desirable to have your pastor present as well. Remember to use a "broken" wooden cross, one that can be taken apart and put back together again, in your home gathering centerpiece. The United Church of Christ's *Book of Worship* includes an order for reconciliation of a penitent person, some or all of which may be used in place of the following ritual.[11]

The Song of Celebration
Sing a hymn of your own choosing, "Lord, Thy Mercy Now Entreating," or the simple "Into My Heart."

The Reading of the Word

After a meal:

All: As our bodies have been fed, O God, now feed our souls on your Word of life.

At other times:

All: May the light of your Word illumine our hearts.

The person who is seeking forgiveness reads Matthew 11:28–30 and Romans 5:6–11.

The Spoken Response

All: Let your Word abide in us and bring hope to our hearts and lives, O God.

The Sung Response

Sing a hymn of your own choosing or sing "Spirit of the Living God," substituting the word "us" for "me" and "Hear us, heal us, fill us, use us" for "Melt me, mold me, fill me, use me."[12]

The Unison Prayer of Confession

All kneel.

All: Hear us, O God. We confess that we have all sinned against you. We confess that we have all sinned against one another. We confess that we have all sinned against ourselves. We come to you broken and in true repentance.

Heal us, O God. Wash away any uncleanness within. Cauterize our wounds. Spread your healing balm on our wounds. Restore all our broken relationships.

Fill us, O God. Pour out your forgiveness. Pour out your shalom, your peace. Pour out your grace. Fill us, until we are filled with your love.

Use us, O God. As *(penitent's name)* now seeks reconciliation, use us to express your caring. Use us to offer your forgiveness. Use us to offer your reconciliation. Use us to offer your love.

The Individual Prayer of Confession

The person who is attempting to deal with his or her sin/brokenness prays, using whatever language is most appropriate.

Penitent: God, be merciful to me, a sinner.

God, be merciful to me, a sinner.

God, be merciful to me, a sinner.

I have sinned against *(name of person)*, and I seek your forgiveness.

I have sinned against *(name of person)*, and I seek to forgive myself.

I have sinned against *(name of person)*, and I seek his/her forgiveness.

Do not be afraid of silences or tears. If the individuals who are in a state of bro-kenness are present and are moved to reconciliation in the midst of the prayers, praise God, from whom all blessings flow.

Penitent: God, be merciful to me, a sinner.

God, be merciful to me, a sinner.

God, be merciful to me, a sinner.

I feel that *(person's name)* has sinned against me.

Anger and hatred burn within my soul.

I seek your help that I may be forgiving.

I feel *(person's name)* has sinned against me.

I am hurt at the core of my soul.

I seek your help that I may be forgiving.

I feel that *(person's name)* has sinned against me.

I cannot find it in my heart to forgive.

I seek your help that I may be forgiving.

Allow the individual to continue as long as he or she feels necessary, being as concrete and specific as possible.

The Assurance of Pardon

If present, the pastor may be asked to lead.

Leader: *(Penitent's name)*, do you believe that God forgives you?

Penitent: I believe.

Leader: Do you forgive yourself?

Penitent: I do, with the help of God.

Leader: Do you forgive all who have sinned against you?

Penitent: I do, with the help of God.

If the alienated individual agrees, continue:

Leader: Do you accept *(person's name)*'s request for forgiveness as sincere?

Penitent: I do.

Leader: Are you willing to forgive *(person's name)*?

Penitent: I am, with the help of God.

Leader: Are you willing to be reconciled to *(person's name)* at this time?

Penitent: I am, with the help of God.

Let the reconciled individuals embrace; join the wooden cross together as a symbol of their forgiveness, their healing, their wholeness in and through Jesus Christ; and then face the group.

The Assurance of Pardon

All others: God loves you. God heals you. God forgives you. We love you. We forgive you. We offer the peace of God to you.

Let all share in passing the peace of God with hugs and kisses.

The Doxology

Stand and join hands in a circle. At the close of the doxology, let those who have been reconciled extinguish the candle.

The Extinguishing of the Candles

Both persons reconciled should lead.

Leaders: May the shalom, the peace, and the reconciliation of God enfold us as the shadows of the night descend upon us.

All: Amen. Amen. Amen.

···Infertility···

One of the most traumatic experiences for a young couple that desire children is not to be able to have them. We offer this particular ritual, which is designed to help the couple place their trust in our loving God, no matter what the outcome. Once again we suggest that you use a wooden cross broken in two pieces for your centerpiece.

If it eventually turns out that having a baby is medically impossible, you may wish to utilize the ritual suggested in the section on pages 61–63, adapting it to your special need.

The Song of Celebration
Sing a hymn of your own choosing or use the following adaptation of "Whisper a Prayer":

> We whisper a prayer in the morning,
> We whisper a prayer at noon,
> We whisper a prayer in the evening,
> "May new life come to us soon."

> *—Traditional; adaptation by Peter Young, 1994*

The Reading of the Word
After a meal:
All: As our bodies have been fed, O God, now feed our souls on your
         Word of life.
At other times:
All: May the light of your Word illumine our hearts.
A good scripture for the occasion is 1 Samuel 1:9–19.

The Response
All: Let your Word abide in us and bring hope to our hearts and lives,
         O God.

The Sharing

It is suggested that your home gathering offerings during this period of hopeful waiting be designated for some organization that deals with the issue of infertility or with adoption.

Leader: Happy are those who consider the poor and those in special need.

The Period of Prayer

Husband and wife place their hands on the woman's abdomen.

Husband and wife: Abraham and Sarah knew the pain of the joy of a new life so longed for yet denied. We join them in that pain and offer our prayer that your love be made manifest in a special way by granting our deepest desire for new life within. Nevertheless, we trust in you and accept your grace for whatever will be. And, as a symbol of this trust, we put this cross together, accepting whatever wholeness you offer. Amen.

Put the cross together, and then, holding hands, wait upon God in a prolonged period of silence.

The Period of Prayer (Alternative)

The following alternative is suggested for insertion in the regular home gathering for as long as you desire. Use whatever you normally will use for prayer, but then add the following as you join the pieces of the cross together:

Husband and wife: In joining these two pieces, we renew our prayer for the wholeness that comes with the gift of new life, and continue to wait upon your grace, accepting whatever wholeness you have to offer. Amen.

The Blessing and Extinguishing of the Candles

The couple hold hands.

Husband and wife: God will bless us and take care of us. God will be kind and gracious to us. God will look on us with favor and will grant us our prayers. Amen.

··· Addiction ···

We have become particularly aware of the number of different aspects of life to which we can become addicted. The usual ones are tobacco, alcohol, gambling, and drugs. But we can become addicted to a wide variety of substances (caffeine/chocolate), or actions (exercise/power), or ideas (religion/conspiracy). Put simply, when there is something other than our own will that controls our actions, we are addicted! By "control" we mean that we are obsessed by, dominated by, haunted by, consumed by the need for the item. If we recognize this, then the daily use of the following ritual may be of some help in breaking the controlling item. Use the broken cross.

The Song of Surrender

Sing verse 1 of "Have Thine Own Way," then enter into a period of prolonged silence in which you lift up the addiction concern.

> Have Thine own way, Lord! Have Thine own way!
> Thou art the Potter; I am the clay.
> Mould me and make me After Thy will,
> While I am waiting, Yielded and still.

> —*Adelaide A. Pollard*

The Reading of the Word

After a meal:

All: As our bodies have been fed, O God, now feed our souls on your Word of life.

At other times:

All: May the light of your Word illumine our hearts.

Read Job 42:1–6.

The Spoken Response

All: Let your Word abide in us and bring hope to our hearts and lives, O God.

The Sung Response

Sing verse 2 of "Have Thine Own Way":

> Have Thine own way, Lord! Have Thine own way!
> Search me and try me, Master, today!
> Whiter than snow, Lord, Wash me just now,
> As in Thy presence Humbly I bow.

The Period of Prayer

Hold hands. Enter into a period of silence. The person with the addiction then offers this prayer, attributed to St. Francis of Assisi:

> Make me an instrument of Thy peace;
> where there is hatred, let me sow love;
> where there is injury, pardon;
> where there is doubt, faith;
> where there is despair, hope;
> where there is darkness, light;
> where there is sadness, joy.
> O Divine Majesty,
> grant that I may not so much seek to be consoled, as to console;
> to be understood as to understand;
> to be loved, as to love;
> for it is in giving that we receive,
> it is in pardoning that we are pardoned,
> and it is in dying that we are born to eternal life.

All: Amen.

The Period of Prayer (Alternative)

The following alternative is suggested for insertion in the regular home gathering for as long as you desire. Use whatever you normally use for prayer, but then add the following as you join the pieces of the cross together:

All: In joining these two pieces, we renew our prayer for help in dealing with (*name the addiction*). We wait upon your grace and wholeness. Amen.

The Song of Surrender

Sing verse 3 of "Have Thine Own Way":

> Have Thine own way, Lord! Have Thine own way!
> Wounded and weary, Help me I pray!
> Power—all power—Surely is Thine!
> Touch me and heal me, Savior divine!

The Words of Confession

There may come a time when the ritual dealing with the overwhelming sense of sin/brokenness and reconciliation is appropriate.

Person with addiction: I confess that *(name the addiction)* has control over my life. I confess that I am powerless in the face of *(name the addiction)*. I confess that I need your help, O God.

All others: We confess that we, too, are powerless in the face of our beloved's addiction. We confess that we, too, need your help, O God.

The Song of Surrender

Sing verse 4 of "Have Thine Own Way":

> Have Thine own way, Lord! Have Thine own way!
> Hold o'er my being Absolute sway!
> Fill with Thy Spirit Till all shall see
> Christ only, always, Living in me.

The Prayer of Surrender

Observe a period of silence. Then pray Reinhold Niebuhr's Serenity Prayer:

All: God, give us grace to accept with serenity the things that cannot be changed, courage to change the things that should be changed, and the wisdom to distinguish the one from the other.

The Extinguishing of the Candles

After a period of silence, put the cross together.

All: Your cross is the sign of shalom, of peace. Your cross is the sign of reconciliation and forgiveness. Your cross is the sign of the power of your presence. In joining this cross we pray that your shalom may enfold us as night descends upon us. Amen.

··· Sexual Violence ···

Individuals subjected to sexual violence, rape, abuse, incest, or molestation share in common the devastating invasion of their personhood. They are also frequently victimized by a conspiracy of silence, born of the mistaken hope that the whole episode will go away. It won't. These persons will never again be the same as they were before the experience. "Sexual violence carries with it a kind of death, and death must be mourned to be truly survived. To disallow victims that mourning period does them no service."[13] Recovery is a long-term process. Feelings of guilt, shame, helplessness, anger, and fear; the loss of self-respect, of self-worth, of security, of self-confidence, and of control over one's own body are only some of the negative feelings that sexual violence brings forth. Those who have been victimized need to be listened to, believed, loved, reassured, and allowed to recover at their own rate, rather than at the family's rate. The ritual that follows is divided into two parts. The first part is suggested for use when the incident(s) of sexual violence are initially discovered or reported. The second part is suggested for long-term use as a part of the regular home gathering ritual. Remember to use the broken cross as the centerpiece, although we suggest that you begin with its pieces joined.

The Song of Healing
Sing, to the tune of Tallis' Canon (1565):

> O God, our pain and hurt we bring
> that you may heal and help us sing.
> Remove our anger and our guilt,
> that broken lives may be rebuilt.

> —*Peter Young, 1996*

The Reading of the Word
After a meal:

All: As our bodies have been fed, O God, now feed our souls on your Word of life.

At other times:

All: May the light of your Word illumine our hearts.

Some suggested readings, depending on your special needs, are Job 3; Psalms 6, 13, 23, or 43; Luke 12:6–7; Romans 8:35–39.

The Response

All: May the light of your Word illumine our hearts and heal our brokenness, O God.

The Sharing

It is suggested that a gift be designated for a women's crisis center or similar organization. You may wish to continue such designation throughout the period that you express this concern in a regular home gathering.

Leader: Happy are those who consider the poor and those in special need.

The Symbolic Act

It is recommended that some symbolic act now take place to express the incident, the anguish that is felt, and the hope for healing. For example, the individual who has been violated may take a large photograph of himself or herself, and cut it up into pieces. Allow the person to express feelings about the effects of the incident on his or her life. At the same time, take the small wooden cross from your centerpiece and break it apart. Place the cut-up picture and the broken cross together in the centerpiece.

The Period of Prayer

It is important to verbalize the incident or incidents of sexual violence that are of concern this day. Even a simple statement of fact, "I was raped yesterday," may be sufficient for the first time you use this ritual. The more the situation can be verbalized, the better, but do not push it.

The person who has been violated expresses the incident of sexual violence in his or her own words.

All: We hear you. We believe you. We love you.

The person who has been violated expresses some of his or her feelings, if possible.

All: We hear you. We believe you. We love you.

Leader: O God, we offer to you the pain, the hurt, the anger, the fear, the helplessness we all feel. Pour out your healing spirit on us all. Help us to walk through this nightmare experience to the dawn of a new day within the sunshine of your love. Enable *(person's name)* to put his/her life back together again.

All: Amen.

The Period of Prayer *(Alternative)*

The following is suggested for insertion in the regular home gathering for as long as is needed. The small wooden cross and the cut-up picture, or whatever other symbol you used, should be kept in the centerpiece. Use your normal procedure; then ask the person who has been sexually violated to put two pieces of the picture together by taping it on the back. At the next family gathering, add another piece; continue until the picture is whole again. As the pieces are joined, the person who has been violated offers a one-sentence prayer such as the following:

Person violated: In joining these two pieces, may the *(name the feeling— anger, fear, hatred, etc.)* I am feeling be touched by your love, and my life come together again.

The Extinguishing of the Candles

All: May the shalom, the peace and the healing of God, enfold us as the shadows of the night descend upon us. May our joining together of the pieces of this cross be as a symbol of our trust and faith in God's grace in this special time of need. Amen.

···Abortion···

We are not concerned here with the pros and cons of abortion, but rather with the difficult decisions that a woman, a family, make around this special concern. Some religious traditions hold that abortion is wrong—period. Some religious traditions hold that abortion is appropriate and sometimes mandated in the case of danger to the mother's health and well-being. Some religious traditions hold that abortion is a decision that a woman alone makes. Since we include dealing with abortion as a part of a home gathering, we see it as a family concern. We suggest that the take-apart wooden cross be used as the centerpiece only because of the potential for brokenness the issue engenders.

The Song of Celebration

Sing "Kum Ba Yah":

> Kum ba yah, my Lord, Kum ba yah!
>   Someone's crying, Lord, Kum ba yah . . .
> Kum ba yah, my Lord, Kum ba yah!
>   Someone's singing, Lord, Kum ba yah . . .
> Kum ba yah, my Lord, Kum ba yah!
>   Someone's praying, Lord, Kum ba yah . . .
> O Lord, Kum ba yah.
>   Come by here, Lord, Come by here . . .

> —*Traditional*

The Reading of the Word

After a meal:

All: As our bodies have been fed, O God, now feed our souls on your Word of life.

At other times:

All: May the light of your Word illumine our hearts.

Suggested scriptures: 1 John 3:19–23; 1 John 4:7–18; or Romans 8:31–39.

The Response

All: Let your Word abide in us as your Spirit guides us in the decisions that lie before us.

The Sharing

It is suggested that a gift be designated to an appropriate organization that deals with abortion, birth, and adoption problems.

Leader: Happy are those who consider the poor and those in special need.

The Period of Prayer

The woman who is pregnant or who has ended her pregnancy holds both parts of the cross in her hands.

Woman: Source from which all life comes and to which all life returns, you know how difficult it is to bring forth life and to give up life. You have brought forth all of creation, but you have given up your Child, as well. You know the pain. You know the anguish of such decision making. So look upon us now in our time of special need. Guide us in our decision making. Bring the broken pieces of our lives together (*join pieces of the cross*), that we may be made whole. Help us to accept whatever decision is made, trusting that your Spirit will guide us.

All join in silent waiting for the guidance of God's Spirit.

The Period of Prayer (Alternative)

The following is suggested for insertion in the regular home gathering for as long as is needed. The small wooden cross should be kept in the centerpiece. Use your normal procedure, then ask the woman who is pregnant or who has ended her pregnancy to offer this prayer at the conclusion of your regular prayer period.

Woman: In joining these two pieces, we continue to ask that your Spirit may guide and direct our continued decision making, that your love may bring our lives together again.

All: Amen.

The Blessing and Extinguishing of the Candles

All: God will bless us and take care of us. God will be kind and gra-
              cious to us. God will look on us with favor, granting us guidance
              and assurance. May the shalom, the peace of God, enfold us as
              the shadows of the night descend upon us. Amen.

··· Suicide ···

The trauma of a suicide is often much greater than a death from natural
causes, because of the deliberate decision that has been made to take one's
own life. All of the normal grief reactions are present and magnified because
of the cloud of unknowing that covers all suicides. We suggest that you set a
"You Are Special" plate in the normal place the individual would sit, and put
on it the broken wooden cross. We also suggest that you use the home gathering for death on pages 56–58, including the use of a candle for each person
present and for the deceased. The following material is designed to be
inserted in that ritual.

Additional Reading from the Word

"How can we tell him the child is dead? He may do himself some harm."
But when David saw that his servants were whispering together, he per-
ceived that the child was dead; and David said to his servants, "Is the
child dead?" They said, "He is dead." Then David rose from the ground,
washed, anointed himself, and changed his clothes. He went into the
house of God, and worshiped; he then went to his own house; and when
he asked, they set food before him and he ate. Then his servants said to
him, "What is this thing that you have done? You fasted and wept for the
child while it was alive; but when the child died, you rose and ate food."

He said, "While the child was still alive, I fasted and wept; for I said,
'Who knows? God may be gracious to me, and the child may live.' But
now he is dead; why should I fast? Can I bring him back again? I shall go
to him, but he will not return to me." (2 Sam. 12:18c–23)

Additions to the Period of Prayer

One member of the family lifts up a "You Are Special" plate and the broken cross.

Leader: Alive and dead, *(deceased's name)* is a special person and will always be special to this family and all who loved him/her. As Christ is the unseen presence at all our meals, so from now on will *(deceased's name)* be an unseen presence. *(Put the cross together.)* As Christ's broken body on the cross made us whole, so do we trust in the cross of God's grace to heal the brokenness of our family and make us whole again. As Christ's broken body was a sign of God's forgiveness, so do we trust in the cross of God's grace to grant us forgiveness.

All: Amen.

Leader: Dear God, in the past weeks, months, years, our lives have changed dramatically. Our loved one made a decision we wish she/he had not made, leaving us heartbroken, with disbelief, guilt, anger, confusion, so many "if-onlys" and "whys." Help us to accept what has happened. Help us to live with only partial answers. Help us to find a way to cherish our memories. Help us to adapt and reorganize our lives. Help us to find a new focus. Help us to respond in a positive way; to go on with renewed faith in your everlasting love.

All: Amen.[14]

···Alzheimer's Disease or AIDS···

Alzheimer's disease is a progressive brain disease that causes dementia and, ultimately, death. Therefore, its diagnosis in a loved one generates incredible trauma. It is frightening to watch a loved one, usually still physically well, wander off into a world of his or her own making, with little or no touch with reality. It is frightening not to be recognized by one's own relative. It is frightening to know that you will more than likely have to place your loved one in a nursing home. AIDS is just as frightening and traumatic. The ritual that follows is designed to be used when a formal diagnosis has been made and the family has to come to grips with the reality of either disease. This is a "You Are Special" plate and wooden cross ritual.

The Song of Faith
Some possible hymns to sing at this time are "My Faith Looks Up to Thee," "He Leadeth Me," or "God Will Take Care of You."

The Reading of the Word
After a meal:

All: As our bodies have been fed, O God, now feed our souls on your Word of life.

At other times:

All: May the light of your Word illumine our hearts.

Suggested passages of scripture are Psalms 23 and 77 and Hebrews 12:1–3.

The Spoken Response
All: Let your Word abide in us and strengthen our faith, O God.

The Sung Response
Sing a hymn of your own choosing or "O Holy Dove of God Descending," which is found in *The New Century Hymnal*.

The Sharing

Pass the pieces of the broken cross around as each person takes a turn in the sharing.

Each participant: The news we received today brings uncertainty to our future, and frightens me because . . .

All, in response: "Why are you cast down, O my soul, and why are you disquieted within me? Hope in God; for I shall again praise my help and my God" (Ps. 42:5).

When the response has been said for the last time, put the cross together and place it in front of the person with the diagnosed disease.

The Period of Prayer

Join hands, go around the table offering one-sentence prayers, and conclude by praying in unison the Prayer of Our Savior.

The Blessing

All present place their hands on the person diagnosed with the disease:

All: God will bless our love for one another all the days of our lives. Amen.

The Period of Prayer (Alternative)

The following prayer is suggested for insertion in the regular home gathering, at the conclusion of the regular prayer period, for as long as is needed. The small wooden cross should be kept in the centerpiece.

All: We join these two pieces of the cross together, continuing to ask for healing and wholeness, but accepting whatever grace you may offer. Amen.

The Extinguishing of the Candles

The person with the diagnosed disease blows out the candle.

All: May the shalom, the peace of God, enfold us as the shadows of night descend upon us. Amen.

Times Related to Our Faith Journey and Church Life

··· Infant Baptism or Dedication ···

There are some rites of passage, times of transition, that are particularly related to our faith community or faith family. The first one is usually infant baptism or dedication. This ceremony recognizes the transition from "outsider" to "insider." (Not that a baby has ever been outside the family of God!) The ceremony, however, formally incorporates both the baby and the parents (particularly new parents) into the faith family. In many homes, the sacrament of Holy Baptism or rite of dedication is often followed by a family gathering for a meal and celebration. It would be appropriate to use this home gathering at that time. If the church presents the child with a baptismal candle, a cradle cross, or some such symbol of the event, use this item in the home gathering centerpiece.

The Song of Celebration
Gather in a circle and sing "Child of Blessing, Child of Promise" or another appropriate song or hymn.

The Reading of the Word
After a meal:

All: As our bodies have been fed, O God, now feed our souls on your Word of life.

At other times:

All: May the light of your Word illumine our hearts.

A suggested passage for this celebration is Romans 6:1–11.

The Spoken Response

All: Let your Word abide in us, O God.

The Sung Response

Sing a hymn of your own choosing or use the following:

Hallelu, hallelu, hallelu, hallelujah! Praise ye the Lord!

For the light of your Word, and our gath'ring together, praise ye
the Lord!

Praise ye the Lord, hallelujah! Praise ye the Lord, hallelujah!

Praise ye the Lord, hallelujah! Praise ye the Lord!

—Traditional; words of second line by Peter Young, 1995

The Sharing

Gifts for the child may be presented or opened at this time.

The Period of Prayer

*At this point, we suggest that one of the parents, holding the baby, sit in a place
that is conveniently and centrally located.*

Leader: We invite you to come, place your hands on the head of (*baby's
name*) and offer a prayer.

*After this has been done, the parents will both place their hands on the child's
head and offer the regular children's blessing.*

The Blessing

*All guests gather in a circle with the parents, their baby, and their other chil-
dren in the center.*

Guests: May Christ be at the center of your lives, even as you are in the
center of the circle of our lives.

All: Amen.

The Extinguishing of the Candles

All: May the shalom, the peace of God, enfold us as the shadows of
the night descend upon us. Amen.

··· First Communion ···

The issue of when an individual should receive First Communion is one on which there is little agreement. In the Orthodox communion, an infant receives First Communion at the time of baptism, and is recognized as a full member of the body of Christ from that moment on. In those congregations that practice believer's baptism, the individual is recognized as a full member of the body of Christ from the time of baptism. In most other Christian groups, however, First Communion is often related to confirmation—when the child/youth confirms the baptism he or she received as an infant. As confirmation has been delayed to an older age, most Protestant communities have had to rethink the meaning of baptism and its relationship to full membership in the body of Christ.

This particular celebration is designed to be used in the home before the child/youth receives communion for the first time, and assumes that the child is not an infant. It is suggested that a chalice of some type and a small dish be used as the focal point of the home gathering centerpiece. This celebration includes an examination. In the ritual as written, we are assuming that both the child and the parents will affirm the child's readiness to participate in the sacrament. In the absence of this affirmation, the celebration should deal with the disappointment as well as the looking forward to a future time when all can affirm the readiness. The child who is to receive First Communion should light the candle.

The Song of Celebration
At the conclusion of the meal, sing "Let Us Talents and Tongues Employ" from *The New Century Hymnal,* or some similar joyful communion hymn.

The Reading of the Word
After a meal:
All: As our bodies have been fed, O God, now feed our souls on your Word of life.
At other times:
All: May the light of your Word illumine our hearts.
A suggested passage for this celebration is 1 Corinthians 11:23–28.

The Spoken Response

All: Let your Word abide in us, O God.

The Sung Response

Sing a hymn of your own choosing or use the following:

> Hallelu, hallelu, hallelu, hallelujah! Praise ye the Lord!
> For the light of your Word, and our gath'ring together, praise ye the
>   Lord!
> Praise ye the Lord, hallelujah! Praise ye the Lord, hallelujah!
> Praise ye the Lord, hallelujah! Praise ye the Lord!

> *—Traditional; words of second line by Peter Young, 1995*

The Time of Examination

Father: Daughter/Son, tomorrow you will receive Holy Communion in the church for the first time. Holy Communion is a solemn, serious event. Would you please tell us, in your own words, why you think it is a serious event.

The child expresses his or her understanding of communion.

Mother: Daughter/Son, tomorrow you will receive Holy Communion in the church for the first time. Holy Communion is not only a solemn event, it is a joyful event. Would you please tell us, in your own words, why you think it is a joyful event.

The child expresses his or her reasons for the joy of communion.

The parents take whatever time they need to discuss the child's understanding of and readiness for communion to their own satisfaction.

Parents: Do you think that you are ready to share in the seriousness and the joy of this occasion with your spiritual family in the church?

The child gives his or her own answer.

The parents place their hands on the child's head.

Parents: May you love God, love yourself, and love your neighbor. May you walk always in the light of Jesus Christ.

The Sharing

Place a gift in the box or container you are currently using in your family.

Leader: Happy are those who consider the poor.

The Extinguishing of the Candles

All: May the shalom, the peace of God, enfold us as the shadows of
the night descend upon us. Amen.

···Confirmation/Affirmation of Baptism/Becoming a Member ···

This celebration is appropriate for use at the time of confirmation, affirmation of baptism, or when a person becomes a member of the church through
some other process. If the individual has had a mentor through the program
of preparation or will have one for the succeeding year, the mentor should be
invited to participate in this celebration. If the family has been using a baptismal candle to celebrate the anniversaries of the baptism, it is appropriate
to include this candle in the home gathering centerpiece. If not, you may
wish to have a framed copy of the baptismal certificate as a part of the centerpiece. A small bowl of water should be available. This is a "You Are Special" plate occasion. Have the individual who is being honored light the
candle.

The Song of Celebration

At the conclusion of the meal, sing "I Was There to Hear Your Borning Cry"
or another appropriate hymn.

The Reading of the Word

After a meal:

All: As our bodies have been fed, O God, now feed our souls on your
Word of life.

At other times:

All: May the light of your Word illumine our hearts.

The scripture is read by a parent or mentor. A suggested passage for this celebration is Matthew 4:18–22.

The Spoken Response

All: Let your Word abide in us, O God.

The Sung Response

Sing a hymn of your own choosing or use the following:

> Hallelu, hallelu, hallelu, hallelujah! Praise ye the Lord!
> For the light of your Word, and our gath'ring together, praise ye the
>   Lord!
> Praise ye the Lord, hallelujah! Praise ye the Lord, hallelujah!
> Praise ye the Lord, hallelujah! Praise ye the Lord!

> *—Traditional; words of second line by Peter Young, 1995*

The Act of Affirmation

The honoree (the one who is to be confirmed, to affirm his or her baptism, or to join the church) stands.

Father: Please light your baptismal candle as an expression of your willingness to affirm anew your life in Christ.

The honoree lights his or her baptismal candle from Christ candle.

Honoree: Christ is the light of the world, and in lighting my baptismal candle, I affirm anew that Christ is the light of my life.

The mother holds up water.

Mother: Out of the waters, God brought forth life. Out of the waters of baptism, God brought forth new life. Let us all affirm the life God has given us.

All present dip their fingers in the water and touch it to their own foreheads.

All: With this water we affirm the life God has given us.

Each person dips his or her fingers into the water and touches it to the forehead of the person to the left.

Each guest: With this water we affirm the new life God has given us in Christ.

Each person dips his or her fingers into the water and touches it to the forehead of the person to the right.

Each guest: With this water we affirm the life God has given us in the community of faith, the church.

Older sibling or other relative: Let us pray. Gracious God, for giving us life, we give you thanks. For giving us new life in Christ through baptism, we give you thanks. For giving us the life of this family, we give you thanks. For giving us life in the community of faith, we give you thanks. For giving us the life of *(mentor's name)*, who has served/will serve as mentor, we give you thanks. For giving to your servant *(honoree's name)* the guidance, the wisdom, and the grace to come to this special moment in his/her life, we give you thanks.

We ask you to bless *(name of person)* in a special way this day. May s/he realize that this decision to affirm his/her baptism and new life in Christ is not the end of the faith journey, but just another milestone along the way.

All: Bind us all together in the name of Christ our Savior, who taught us to pray together.

Pray the Prayer of Our Savior.

The Blessing

All present gather around and place their hands on the one being honored.

All: May you love God, love yourself, love your neighbor. May you walk always in the light of Jesus Christ. Amen.

The Sharing

The one being honored indicates the recipient of tonight's gifts.

Honoree: Happy are those who consider the poor.

The Extinguishing of the Candles

Allow the one who is being honored to extinguish both candles.

All: May the shalom, the peace of God, enfold us as we continue our faith journeys together. Amen.

··· Church Office, Special Recognition, Licensing, Commissioning, or Ordination ···

In the course of our faith journey within a particular community of faith, we are often elected to a particular office or are singled out for special recognition and honor. This may be as an officer of a youth group, of some other organization within the church, or of the church as a whole. Perhaps the congregation has held a time of special recognition for length of service or perfect attendance at church school. An honor may have been bestowed by the community or wider church. Perhaps a member of the family has been licensed, commissioned, or ordained to ministry. These are "You Are Special" plate occasions, times of special joy and celebration, and should be recognized appropriately within the family itself. Let the honoree light the candle to begin the home gathering.

The Song of Celebration

Choose the honoree's favorite song or hymn, choose a song that seems to fit the reason for the honor, or sing "Called as Partners in Christ's Service" from *The New Century Hymnal.*

The Reading of the Word

After a meal:

All: As our bodies have been fed, O God, now feed our souls on your Word of life.

At other times:

All: May the light of your Word illumine our hearts.

Suggested scriptures are Isaiah 6:1–8, Mark 1:14–20, or Philippians 3:12–14.

The Spoken Response

All: Let your Word abide in us, O God.

The Sung Response

Sing a hymn of your own choosing or use the following:

> Hallelu, hallelu, hallelu, hallelujah! Praise ye the Lord!
> For the light of your Word, and our gath'ring together, praise ye
>   the Lord!
> Praise ye the Lord, hallelujah! Praise ye the Lord, hallelujah!
> Praise ye the Lord, hallelujah! Praise ye the Lord!

> *—Traditional; words of second line by Peter Young, 1995*

The Sharing

The one being honored designates the recipient of tonight's gifts.

Honoree: Happy are those who consider the poor.

The Time of Special Recognition

Leader: This is a special time in the life of our loved one, *(person's name)*. Having been honored by *(indicate reason for occasion)*, we share in the joy of this time. We would also like to honor *(person's name)* in our own way this night.

Guest 1:   First, a little cheer.

Shout "Hip, Hip, Hoorah!" or another familiar cheer. Enjoy!

Guest 2:   Now, a little song.

Sing "For S/he's a Jolly Good Person."

Guest 3:   And now a toast.

Using a glass of juice or wine, as may be appropriate for your family, let each person present offer a special toast to the honoree.

Leader: Finally, we would like to present you with a special gift in recognition of the honor bestowed upon you.

This gift can be a serious one or a fun one, purchased or made. It can also be the honoree's favorite dessert. Make it special; make it joyous.

The Period of Prayer

Leader: Thank you, O wonderful God, for the joy you have brought to our family through the honoring of *(person's name)*. We thank you that s/he has been able to serve the community of faith in this way and to bring honor to your holy name.

We thank you that *(person's name)* is a part of our family and that we all together are a part of a larger family, our special faith community. We thank you that this larger family has so honored our loved one.

We pray that s/he and we may continue to be faithful servants in your service, in the service of our church, in the service of all peoples. In Christ's name.

All: Amen

The Blessing

All present form a circle, with the honoree in the center. They place their hands on his or her head.

All: May you love God, love yourself, love your neighbor. May you walk always in the light of Jesus Christ.

Honoree: May our love for one another grow stronger day by day.

All: Amen.

The Extinguishing of the Candles

The honoree blows out the candle.

Honoree: May the shalom, the peace of God, enfold us as the shadows of the night descend upon us.

All: Amen.

Celebrations of **P**reparation for the Church Gathering

··· Advent and Christmas Eve ···

The home family in *Celebrate Life* uses a large white Christ candle surrounded by four traditional Advent candles on an Advent wreath as its centerpiece. The Advent candle or candles are lit only during the celebration of preparation for the particular Sunday in Advent. The Christ candle is lit every night. Advent has been observed in the church since the fourth century. It was initially seen as a period of repentance and preparation for baptisms, which were traditionally held on Epiphany Sunday. Advent was later changed to focus on the coming of the Christ—his birth, his second coming. It begins on the fourth Sunday before Christmas and ends on Christmas Eve.

The Lighting of the Christ Candle
All: Christ is the light of the world. Christ is the light of our lives.

The Blessing
If not at a meal, eliminate this blessing.
All: In praise of you, O God, we break this bread (*break a piece of bread*), for by your gracious coming, we all have been fed.
Share bread with all present.

The Song of Celebration
Sing an Advent hymn or Christmas carols.

The Reading of the Word

Reader: May the light of your Word prepare our hearts for the coming of the Christ.

Scripture readings for each week in Advent may be found in the *Revised Common Lectionary* of your church. If this is not available, the following suggestions are made:

First week in Advent: Isaiah 40:1–5 and Matthew 3:1–6.

Second week in Advent: Isaiah 61:1–4 and Luke 4:16–21.

Third week in Advent: Isaiah 9:2–7 and Luke 1:46–55.

Fourth week in Advent: Isaiah 11:1–9 and Luke 2:22–32.

Christmas Eve: Luke 1:26–33 and John 1:1–14.

The Sung Response

To the tune of "O Come, O Come, Emmanuel," sing:

O come, O come, dear Jesus Christ,

and dwell within our hearts this night,

that love and peace and joy may be ours,

with hope to fill our waiting hours.

O come, O come, dear Jesus Christ,

and bless us with eternal light.

—Peter Young, 1996

The Sharing

These gifts may be designated for your congregation's special Christmas offering or appeal or to whatever your family has chosen for the year.

Father: Happy are those who consider the poor.

Gifts are then given.

The Period of Advent Preparation and Prayer

Many families have traditions that may be used at this time. Some may use an Advent calendar that includes readings and other activities. Alternatives, a nonprofit organization located in Ellenwood, Georgia, provides a number of resources that do not further the commercialization of Christmas. Design your own ritual, or use the following.

First Week

Child: I now light the first candle in our Advent wreath. This stands for preparation. What are some of the ways we want to prepare for the coming of Jesus this year?

Each member of the family offers one or more suggestions. You may wish to include some spiritual preparation, a schedule for decorating your home, baking cookies to share with shut-ins or others, and making some special decoration.

Second Week

Child: I now light the second candle in our Advent wreath. This stands for hope. What are some of the ways Jesus has brought hope to our family? What are some of the ways we can help bring hope to someone else?

Each member of the family offers one or more suggestions. This is a good time for parents to talk about their own faith to the children. The family may decide to read to a shut-in, deliver Meals on Wheels, or invite a person who lives alone to share a meal with you on a regular basis.

Third Week

Mother: I now light the third candle in our Advent wreath. This stands for joy. What are some of the ways Jesus has brought joy to our lives? What are some of the things that really make us happy? Is there any way that we can help someone else to be joyful?

Each member of the family offers one or more suggestions. Joy is different from hope: joy is pleasure; hope is expectation of something better. The family may decide to dress up as elves and deliver gifts to a nursing home or hospital, or to others in need.

Fourth Week

Father: I now light the fourth candle in our Advent wreath. This stands for peace. What are some ways that Jesus has given us peace? What are some things we can do to share the peace of Christ?

Each family member offers one or more suggestions to help the family realize that peace begins in our own hearts and then moves like ripples on a pond to the family, the community, the nation, and the world. You may wish to make a commitment to select from the newspaper a situation where there is no peace, and to pray for the people there in your family gathering each week.

Christmas Eve

Do not light the Christ candle at the beginning.

Family member: I now light all of the Advent candles and the Christ candle. Our preparations are over. We have received hope, joy, and peace in our lives. Now love comes down to us in Jesus Christ. As Jesus taught us, Let us love one another, even as Jesus loves us.

Closing Prayer

Close each week with this prayer, substituting the theme for the week.

All: During this Advent season, most gracious God, keep us focused on the coming of Jesus Christ to this world and to our lives. May the hustle and bustle of the commercial preparation for Christmas not distract us from realizing that Jesus really is the reason for the season. During this week ahead, help us to focus especially on:

Week 1:	The preparation of our hearts.
Week 2:	The hope that Jesus Christ has brought to our lives.
Week 3:	The joy that Jesus has given us.
Week 4:	The peace that Jesus Christ offers us and the world.
Christmas Eve:	The thoughts expressed in the following prayer:

O Love that has come in Jesus our Christ,
be born anew in us this night.
Be born anew and grow afresh,
that our lives may reflect your glorious light. Amen.

The Blessing

Parents place their hands on the heads of the children.

Parents: May you love God, love yourself, love your neighbor. May you walk always in the light of Jesus Christ.

Children hold hands with their parents.

Children: May our love for one another grow stronger day by day.

All: Amen.

The Extinguishing of the Candles

All: May the shalom, the peace of God, enfold us as the shadows of the night descend upon us. Amen.

··· Lent, including Ash Wednesday ···

The home family in *Celebrate Life* uses a large purple candle as the Christ candle, with a large wooden cross behind it. Many traditions have grown up surrounding the preparation for and the observance of the Lenten season of the church year.

Some of these traditions are related to food: feasting prior to Lent, fasting during Lent. Public Mardi Gras, or "Fat Tuesday," celebrations often mark the beginning of Lent. Some communities observe Shrovetide—the Sunday, Monday, and Tuesday prior to Lent—as a time of both confession and festivities. Individual families carry on the tradition of having doughnuts or pancakes on Shrove Tuesday.

Christians traditionally relate the forty days of Lent (not counting Sundays) to the forty days Jesus spent in the wilderness at the outset of his public ministry. Because the Jewish Passover celebration usually falls during this period, there is also a conscious connection with the forty years of Exodus wandering.

Ash Wednesday has been a traditional day of penitence and fasting as the Lenten season begins. It has been marked by the burning of palm branches from the previous year's Palm Sunday and the placing of ashes on the forehead of the penitent. This is a recognition that it is from the dust we have come and to the dust we will return. Only by the grace of God do we have life, and that eternal in the Risen Christ.

It is suggested that this home gathering celebration take place sometime during Shrovetide.

The Song of Penitence

Sing a hymn expressing sorrow for our sin and for the hope of salvation, such as "My Faith Looks Up to Thee."

The Reading of the Word

After a meal:

All: As our bodies have been fed, O God, now feed our souls on your Word of life.

At other times:

All: May the light of your Word illumine our hearts.

A suggested scripture is Matthew 4:1–11.

The Spoken Response

All: Let your Word abide in us throughout this Lenten season, O God.

The Preparation for Lent/Family Lenten Discipline

Leader: As disciples of Jesus Christ, we are called to struggle against everything that leads us away from the love of God and neighbor. Repentance, fasting, prayer, study, and works of love help us to return to the love of God and neighbor. Let us, therefore, commit ourselves anew to love God, neighbor, and self through confessing our sin and establishing our Lenten discipline.

Observe a period of silence for personal prayers of confession.

All: We confess that we have not loved you with all our hearts, and minds, and strength. We confess that we have not loved our neighbors as ourselves. We confess that we have not forgiven others as we have been forgiven. Have mercy on us, O God, and grant us your peace. Amen.

Allow time for individual members of the family to give thought to which Lenten discipline they will establish for themselves. Have them write their choices on a thin piece of paper. Then discuss what you will do as a family in the way of a Lenten discipline. (Remember that the main areas of discipline are repentance, fasting, prayer, study, and works of love.) Write the family discipline on a thin piece of paper also. Place all the slips of paper in a bowl. Touch the candle to the slips. When the paper has turned to ashes, have someone offer the following prayer.

Leader: God, bless these ashes by which we show that we are dust. Pardon our sins and keep us faithful to the discipline of Lent, for you do not want sinners to die but to live with the risen Christ, who reigns with you for ever and ever.

All: Amen.

Some families may wish to mark the foreheads of all present with the ashes. The ashes should remain on through Ash Wednesday as a reminder of the Lenten discipline to which the individual and the family are committed. Or the family may wish to keep the ashes until Ash Wednesday and then mark the foreheads for the day.

The Sharing

Use Lenten coin folders or some similar container for your gifts during this special season. If possible, let it be for a cause related to your family discipline.

Leader: Happy are those who consider the poor.

The Blessing

Parents place their hands on the heads of the children.

Parents: May you love God, love yourself, love your neighbor. May you walk always in the light of Jesus Christ.

Children hold hands with their parents.

Children: May our love for one another grow stronger day by day.

All: Amen.

If no children are present, everyone may say the blessing:

All: God bless you and take care of you. God be kind and gracious to you. God look on you with favor and give you peace. Amen.

The Extinguishing of the Candle

All: May the shalom, the peace of God, enfold us as we begin our Lenten journey to the cross and the empty tomb. Amen.

··· Palm Sunday and Holy Week ···

The only change that the home family in *Celebrate Life* makes to the center-piece is to add a palm from the previous year's Palm Sunday. Palm Sunday marks the beginning of Holy Week, one of the most dramatic times in the life of the church. The long penitential journey is drawing to a close. The focus moves from the ministry of Jesus to the concluding events of his life on earth. This celebration of preparation helps to highlight the events of Holy Week, ending with the crucifixion and burial of Jesus.

The Song of Celebration

It is suggested that you sing "Ride On! Ride On in Majesty."

The Reading of the Word in Preparation for Palm Sunday and Holy Week

After a meal:

All: As our bodies have been fed, O God, now feed our souls on your Word of life.

At other times:

All: May the light of your Word illumine our hearts.

Members of the family take turns reading all of the following passages, which reflect the events of Holy Week:

Palm Sunday:	John 12:12–15.
Holy Monday:	Mark 11:15–1.
Holy Tuesday:	John 12:20–27.
Holy Wednesday:	Luke 22:3–6.
Maundy Thursday:	John 18:15–18.
Good Friday:	John 19:17–30.

Follow each day's reading with silent meditation.

The Spoken Response

All: Let your Word abide in us, O God.

The Sung Response

It is suggested that you sing "Were You There?," a familiar spiritual.

The Sharing

Continue with whatever purpose of giving you have used during Lent.

Leader: Happy are those who consider the poor.

The Period of Prayer

Join hands. Let each member of the family offer a one-sentence prayer. Conclude with this modification of the prayer of preparation for Sunday:

Leader: We praise and thank you, O God, that you have not left us alone in this world. We thank you that we do not have to rely on our own strength or resources. You have called us to be part of the community of faith, the church, our church. You have called us to be members one of another with all who share in the resurrection faith. You have called us to worship and to serve as one in the body of Christ. Prepare our hearts for this most holy of weeks, which we are about to observe with our sisters and brothers in Christ. Blessed be your name, O God, forever and ever.

All: Amen.

The Blessing

Parents place their hands on the heads of the children.

Parents: May you love God, love yourself, love your neighbor. May you walk always in the light of Jesus Christ.

Children hold hands with their parents.

Children: May our love for one another grow stronger day by day.

All: Amen.

If no children are present, everyone may say the blessing:

All: God bless you and take care of you. God be kind and gracious to you. God look on you with favor and give you peace. Amen.

The Extinguishing of the Candles

Leader: May the shalom, the peace of God, enfold us as we begin our journey from Palm Sunday to the cross.

All: Amen.

···Easter···

It is suggested that this particular celebration take place on the Saturday prior to Easter. The family may wish to make Easter egg decorating a part of the celebration, so make sure that you have all necessary materials on hand. Begin with the centerpiece as it has been during Lent. The Easter season continues from Easter Sunday to Pentecost Sunday, one of the most joyous and festive seasons of the church year. This is a special time for resurrection people. As *The Handbook of the Christian Year* puts it, "These Sundays (following Easter) are not only the Lord's Day, they are in the season that is to the rest of the Christian Year what the Lord's Day is to the week."[15]

The Song of Celebration

Sing verse 1 of "Were You There?" ("Were you there when they crucified my Lord?").

The Reading of the Word

After a meal:

As our bodies have been fed, O God, now feed our souls on your Word of life.

At other times:

All: May the light of your Word illumine our hearts.

Read the passage of scripture you find most appropriate. We suggest that you vary the texts each year:

Year 1:   Matthew 27:32–54.

Year 2:   Mark 15:33–47.

Year 3:   Luke 23:13–25.

Year 4:   John 19:17–30.

The Song of Celebration

Sing verse 2 of "Were You There?" ("Were you there when they nailed him to the tree?").

The Review of the Family Lenten Discipline in Preparation for Easter

Leader: As disciples of Jesus Christ, we were called to struggle against everything that leads us away from the love of God and neighbor during this Lenten season. Among the disciplines we were encouraged to undertake were repentance, fasting, prayer, study, and works of love. Let us take a few moments to measure our lives against the discipline to which we committed ourselves at the beginning of Lent.

All share a time of silent contemplation.

The Song of Celebration and Prayer of Confession

Sing verse 3 of "Were You There?" ("Were you there when they laid him in the tomb?").

All: We confess that we have not loved you with all our hearts, and minds, and strength through this Lenten season. We confess that we have not loved our neighbors as ourselves through this Lenten season. We confess that we have not forgiven others as we have been forgiven through this Lenten season. Have mercy on us, O God, bury our sins with Christ in the tomb, and grant us your peace. Amen.

The Reading of the Word

If you are reading the scriptures as indicated above, then read:

    Year 1:   Matthew 28:1–8.
    Year 2:   Mark 16:1–8.
    Year 3:   Luke 24:1–12.
    Year 4:   John 20:1–18.

The Song of Celebration

Sing verse 4 of "Were You There?" ("Were you there when he rose up from the grave?").

The Sharing

Place a gift in whatever envelope or container your church has provided for a special Easter offering.

Leader: Happy are those who consider the poor.

The Blessing

Parents place their hands on the heads of the children.

Parents: May you love God, love yourself, love your neighbor. May you walk always in the light of Jesus Christ.

Children hold hands with their parents.

Children: May our love for one another grow stronger day by day.

All: Amen.

If no children are present, everyone may say the blessing:

All: God bless you and take care of you. God be kind and gracious to you. God look on you with favor and give you peace. Amen.

The Extinguishing of the Candle

Before extinguishing the candle, remove the cross and any other items around it. Place a butterfly or some other symbol of resurrection in its place. When the candle is extinguished, replace it with a white candle.

All: May the shalom, the peace of God, enfold us as we end our Lenten journey to the cross, and to the empty tomb. May the blessings of Easter be ours, now and always. Amen.

Celebratory Rituals for the
Church

[The tension between religious education and liturgy has not always been creative,] but the matter of seeing worship as profoundly educative or of seeing religious education as profoundly significant for worship has only more recently broken through in Protestantism.

There is now an attempt to relate the liturgical celebrations within the Christian year and the sacramental celebrations from birth to death to the educational experiences which prepare persons not only to understand and to participate in them, but also to critique and renew these liturgical events so that they are genuinely humanizing and life-giving rather than deadening or life-denying.

—*Robert L. Browning and Roy A. Reed*[1]

The Church Gathering as Central

In this part of *Celebrate Life,* we are not concerned with duplicating the standard rituals, rites, and sacraments being used in the church. Rather, we are concerned with rituals that bridge the gap between home and church. As noted in the preface, the church has often been more interested in maintaining itself as an institution than it has been in supporting and empowering its members in their passage though life.

In spite of its professed belief in the "priesthood of all believers," the church has basically emphasized the sense of "call" to the ordained ministry. It has done this in its preaching, in its teaching, and in its rituals. As Browning and Reed point out in *The Sacraments in Religious Education and Liturgy,* "laity have little preparation, educationally, and no high moment of decision, liturgically, that publicly celebrates the unique focus of their universal priesthood in a particular occupational or voluntary expression."[2]

Thus, the gap continues to widen!

If the church is our "larger family" in Christ, if Paul is correct in his analogy of the church as the body of Christ and we are individually members of it, then the church has to be concerned about all of its parts, and its parts have to be concerned with the whole body. This means that the church gathering in worship is central to its own life and to the life of its members. We do not discount education, community, service, or any other aspect of the church's life and ministry, but worship is the heartbeat of the community of faith.

Bishop John Spong put his finger on it when trying to explain how an experience is transmitted from the person who has it to others. He was speaking about the resurrection, and that is very appropriate here, for if the community of faith isn't a resurrection people, it is nothing. He writes:

> When a person experiences a transforming reality, one filled with integrity and incapable of being denied, that experience has to be processed. The processing involves first recalling, reliving, and re-creating the context, and varied attempts, usually in a liturgical or ceremonial format, to revisit the moment. In time this experience is described, understood, and interpreted within the context of the life of the processing one or the processing community. In this way the transforming reality passes into the history of the people, tribe, nation, and civilization of which this person is a member.[3]

"My major concern for the Church," writes Marva Dawn, "has to do with worship, because its character-forming potential is so subtle and barely noticed, and yet worship creates a great impact on the hearts and minds and lives of a congregation's members. Indeed, how we worship both reveals and forms our identity as persons and communities."[4]

The church's worship generates an identity that is readily discerned even by strangers who walk through the door! That is because, for whatever reason, the community exudes an aura. It may be an aura of anger, hatred, distrust, fear, dissension, or it may be an aura of acceptance, warmth, trust, forgiveness. It comes from the way people experience these realities and see them as relating to their own lives or not!

The church gathering is the place where the experiences of the transforming reality of the presence of God are celebrated, processed, recalled, relived, re-created, and revisited—not only by the professional clergy, but by all members of the body of Christ. When the church gathering generates an atmosphere that reflects the accepting, forgiving, reconciling grace of God, its members pass along the transforming reality of these experiences to their everyday living. It is then that the priesthood of all believers means something.

Celebratory Rituals for the Church

Therefore, it is very important for the affirmation of this priesthood that each local congregation recognize the milestones, the times of joy, the times of transition, and the times of trauma in the lives of its members—those significant events for which we have provided home gathering rituals in the first part of *Celebrate Life*. As with the home gathering rituals, the recognition best takes place in the context of the regular church gathering, whether it is for worship or for community-building. In addition, the local church should give consideration to developing special ways of recognizing special times within the institutional life of the church—for example, special recognition when a person joins the church, when a person moves from cradle roll into Sunday church school, when a family moves, or the like.

Each local church usually provides for an opportunity, at some point in the worship, to welcome visitors, make announcements, and/or request prayer concerns. In the rituals that follow, such times are called "the gathering." The gathering is a time to welcome visitors; recognize milestones; recognize times of joy, transition, trauma; and to lift up any concerns of the congregation.

In her *Women Who Run with the Wolves,* Clarissa Estés made a statement that goes to the heart of what the church should be all about. You see, so many of us simply get by in life, we simply survive. Estés said, "Now is the time to go to the next stage after survivorship, to healing and *thriving.*"[5] Now is the time for the church to help us recover the joy and zest in living as a resurrection people, to move from survivorship to healing to thriving!

Celebrating Milestones and Other Special Times in the Lives of Members

The categories that we are using are slightly different from the categories in the first part of the book simply because not all of the special times one might celebrate in a home gathering are appropriate for the church gathering. Many times, such as those in the category of times of special concern, are very private times. A person or family may lift these up in a prayer concern during worship, but it is more likely a time when a pastor will represent the larger church family in sharing together privately. You will quickly note that the celebratory rituals are frequently quite simple and may consist of nothing more than a symbol and a noting of the special time as a prayer concern (joyous or otherwise). During the period of prayer, a pastor could light a candle of shalom (peace, healing, wholeness) and speak aloud the names of the persons for whom prayers have been asked during the gathering time. This, too, is something quite simple, but it plays a very important role in bridging the gap between church and home.

··· Engagement ···

In the context of worship. An engagement may be shared with the congregation during the gathering. It becomes a joyful prayer concern. When it is known in advance, the couple may be presented with a copy of an appropriate marriage booklet.

In the context of community. The women of the congregation may hold a shower for the engaged couple.

In private. All couples who plan to be married at the church should participate in premarital counseling with the pastor.

··· Marriage ···

In the context of worship. On the Sunday following the wedding, the couple should be lifted up for prayer during the gathering. On the first appearance of the newly married couple in worship, they could be asked to read the morning scripture lessons or participate in some other meaningful manner.

In the context of community. Sometimes, when a couple have been married at a distance and have returned home for a first visit, their family could hold a special coffee following worship. This would provide everyone with an opportunity to extend greetings.

··· Birth or Adoption ···

In the context of worship. Whenever a child is born to a member of the congregation or whenever one is adopted, a red rose could be placed on the altar the following Sunday. The child and the family would then be lifted up in a joyous prayer concern. The birth of a grandchild or great-grandchild may be similarly announced during the gathering and become a joyous prayer concern.

In private. Children from birth to age three are often placed on the cradle roll. A series of parenting letters may be sent at stated intervals, as well as birthday cards, by a cradle roll superintendent to emphasize the bridge between home and church.

··· Birthdays and Anniversaries ···

In the context of worship. Some congregations include the names of individuals having birthdays and anniversaries during the coming week in the pastoral prayer, along with other prayer requests. Some congregations recognize the special milestone of a child's third birthday by presenting him or her with a children's Bible during the gathering. On the occasion of special birthdays, the event may be recognized by having the individual read the morning scripture lessons. Couples having anniversaries may asked to read the lessons in recognition of the occasion.

In the context of community. Often congregations will recognize all birthdays and anniversaries during a coffee hour. "Happy Birthday/Anniversary" is sung to each individually. Parents of young children sometimes have a birthday party for their child and provide a birthday cake for all to share. Family members sometimes have a special coffee (featuring tablecloths, punch bowl, silver service, decorated cake, etc.) to honor their parents on special anniversaries (for example, the twenty-fifth or fiftieth). When elderly or homebound members have a birthday, a congregation might provide cards to be signed by all present and sent to them.

In private. As simple as it may seem, a birthday or anniversary card sent to all members and friends of the congregation is often deeply appreciated. If the birthdays and anniversaries are printed in the bulletin for the week or newsletter for the month, members can be encouraged to offer a prayer for each person on the day of the birthday or anniversary.

··· Graduation ···

In the context of worship. Individuals graduating from high school, college, or graduate school may also be honored at a service of worship. Each graduate may be asked to lead a portion of the service. After the sermon, the following little ritual could be used.

Pastor: On behalf of the members and friends of this congregation, we congratulate you on successfully reaching this next step on your journey through life. As you continue your journey, as important as your particular chosen field may be, what is more important is that your life, as a follower of Jesus Christ, continue to reflect his presence and love in all your endeavors. I challenge you to so live. Will you accept that challenge?

Graduates: Trusting in the grace and strength of God, I accept.

Pastor: Accept this small gift as a token of our love and support.

An appropriate devotional booklet is presented on behalf of the congregation.

In the context of community. A special coffee could then be held following the worship. A small basket may be decorated for each graduate. Cards and congratulatory gifts could be placed in these baskets by the members and friends of the congregation.

··· Promotion or Special Honor ···

In the context of worship. Promotion and special honors granted to members of the congregation may be lifted up as joys during the gathering. The individual may be asked to read the morning scripture lessons or participate in some other appropriate manner.

In the context of community. Depending on the circumstances and the individuals involved, their families may wish to hold a special coffee for the occasion.

···New Home Blessing···

This particular ritual would take place in the new home instead of during morning worship or community. Members of the congregation and friends of the family would be invited to attend the home blessing celebration.

The family places an unlit candle in each room of the house in advance of the gathering.

Pastor: May the shalom, the peace of God, be on all who enter here.

All: Amen.

Pastor: We gather today to rejoice with (*name of the couple and family*) on the completion of their new home. We also gather as friends and members of their spiritual family to ask God's special blessings upon this home and family.

Father: Abraham, heeding God's call, took his family and all that he owned, and walked by faith. The disciples, heeding Christ's call, left all that they had, and followed him by faith. We have come to this new home (and new community) in response to God's call. We come by faith and in faith.

The mother places the Christ candle from the church in a selected place.

Mother: We place this Christ candle from our community of faith in the midst of our home. We will light this candle in recognition of the fact that while we walk by faith, we do not walk alone.

The mother lights the Christ candle.

All: Christ is the light of the world. Christ is the light of our lives.

Daughter: Let us carry the light into all the rooms in our home, that Christ may truly be the light of this home for all who dwell here.

Pastor: Starting with the members of the family, we will take turns lighting a candle from the Christ candle and offering a simple prayer of blessing. When we have blessed each room, we will return to this location.

Family member (lighting candle and choosing one of the following blessings or creating one): "May this kitchen bring warmth and joy to all" or "May this bedroom bring peaceful rest" or similar words of blessing.

After completing the blessings, all return to the central location.

All: (*Sing the Doxology*) Praise God from whom all blessings flow . . .

Pastor: On behalf of your larger family, your community of faith, we present you with this cross. Let us pray. Gracious God, fill this home with your love. Gracious God, fill this home with your peace. Gracious God, fill this home with your grace. Gracious God, fill this home with your forgiveness. Gracious God, fill this home with your presence, today and always. Through Christ our Savior.

All: Amen.

··· Separation/Return ···

In the context of worship. There are several types of separations that take place within the life of a congregation. One has already been mentioned as being a milestone: graduation. But there are others that should be recognized in appropriate ways, and always in prayer.

For example, when young people attend summer camp, they experience significant times of separation and of return. The young people should know that they go with the blessing of the congregation. They represent the congregation there. They are different persons when they return. When they return, they should be asked to share their experience with the congregation.

The same is true of young people attending regional and/or national youth events sponsored by their denomination. It also applies to individuals from the church who represent the congregation at various gatherings of the denomination.

On these occasions, an order of recognition similar to the one given below can be used. These should be more or less elaborate depending on the circumstances. The sharing of the experience upon return is an important connection between the individual experience and the corporate body the individual represents, and it should be done at an appropriate point in a worship service.

An Order of Recognition for a Youth Delegate

This order for a youth delegate, developed by Douglas Fauth, was created for someone who was to attend a United Church of Christ national youth event. The introductory words were adapted from the "Order for Affirmation of Ministry" from the UCC's Book of Worship.[6]

Pastor: Brothers and sisters in Christ, *(delegate's name)*, grace, peace, and mercy to you from Jesus Christ. There are different kinds of spiritual gifts, but the same Spirit gives them. There are different ways of serving, but the same God is served. There are different abilities to perform service, but the same God gives ability to each of us for our particular service. The Spirit's presence is shown in some way in each person for the good of all. Christ is like a single body which has many parts. If one part suffers, all the other parts suffer with it; if one part is praised, all the other parts share its happiness. All of us are Christ's body, and each one is a part of it. One in the body, One in the Spirit, sharing many gifts.

One in the Spirit. "Sharing Many Gifts" was the theme of the 1996 national youth event of the United Church of Christ. *(Delegate's name)*, we, your friends and family at Mayville Congregational United Church of Christ, want to send you with our blessing and officially recognize that you are going on a special (long!) journey. We want to share with you our strength, our faith, and our love.

Will the congregation please stand and affirm together the faith by which *(delegate's name)* is being sent, using the statement of faith of the United Church of Christ.

All stand and repeat the statement of faith.

Pastor: *(Delegate's name)*, I have three simple questions to ask you. Do you promise to share, as best you are able, in the spirit and the oneness you find at the national youth event?

Delegate: I do.

Pastor: Do you promise to minister to us, when you return, by telling us about the event, and sharing the good experiences from it?

Delegate: I do.

Pastor:	And, finally—and this may be the most important question of all—do you promise to try really hard to have a good time, respecting those with whom you will travel and live?
Delegate:	I do.
Pastor:	I ask that you stand and reach out your hands toward (delegate's name) as a sign of blessing. The children and I will form a circle, with (delegate's name) in the middle. We will pray with the ancient sign of the church, the laying on of hands. This is one of the oldest ways of offering someone our blessing.

Let us pray: Almighty God, strengthen by your Holy Spirit (delegate's name) for the ministry and encounter with your wider church at the national youth event. Give to him/her every good, to be a blessing to others, to be a blessing to this congregation, and to have a really good time. This we pray, as one in the Spirit with the youth and those of all ages in the United Church of Christ.

| All: | Amen. |

A small gift of a pin with the logo of the Youth Event is then given to the individual, with the blessings of the congregation.

Other Types of Separation

Some separations are much more serious in nature, signifying a major change in the life of the member. This may be entering military service, being called up for active National Guard duty, or entering a nursing home. Try to give an appropriate gift of remembrance to such individuals. For those going on active duty or into the service, the gift may be a New Testament and Psalms. For those entering a nursing home, it may be a picture of the church.

While an individual is on active duty—particularly where there is a dangerous situation, as in the Gulf War—the names of these individuals, as well as others known to the congregation, may be listed in the bulletin as a part of the silent prayer offered during the lighting of the candle of shalom:

> Where there is peace in the heart, there is peace in the home. When there is peace in the home, there is peace in the community. When there is peace in the community, there is peace in the nation. When there is

peace in the nation, there is peace in the world. We pray for peace. We pray that it may begin with us. This day in particular we pray for peace in the Middle East, remembering in a special way (*names of the individuals*).

When an individual returns from the service or active duty, a yellow rose may be placed on the altar.

In private. Daily devotional guides should be distributed on a regular basis to shut-ins and people in nursing homes by members of the church, rather than by the pastor. These folks should also be remembered at other times of the year. For example, during Advent, baskets put together at an Advent workshop may be taken to them; on Palm Sunday, palms from the church may be shared.

··· Retirement ···

In the context of worship. Recognition of retirement may take place in a variety of ways. During the gathering, notice could be made of the retirement as a special prayer concern for the day. The individual may be asked to read the morning scripture lessons. If the person who is retiring is leaving the community, the ritual entitled "When a Member Moves" (page 140) could be used. If the retirement is from a long-held position in the church, then a small gift representative of the position held is suggested, a token of thanksgiving from the congregation.

In the context of community. A special coffee is often held in connection with retirements.

Celebrating Times of Trauma

···Health and Expressed Special Concerns···

In the context of worship. Usually any serious accident, illness, or hospitalization is mentioned as a prayer concern during the gathering, unless the individual or family specifically requests otherwise. Many of the situations dealt with in the first part of the book as times of uncertainty and times of special concern are very private in nature, and may never be lifted up in worship as a prayer concern. Always be careful to respect this privacy, and only lift up the concern if the family or individual involved specifically requests it.

More and more congregations are offering rituals of healing, either as a part of the regular worship or as special services. The United Church of Christ's *Book of Worship* (1986) contains such a service.

In private. A flower, such as a single carnation, could be taken to any member or friend of the congregation who is hospitalized. A booklet such as *Looking Up . . . While Lying Down* or *Color Me Well,* or any other appropriate material, may also presented to the individual or family concerned.[7] It is important to provide something tangible as a representation of the prayers and support of the community of faith. The *Book of Worship,* mentioned above, also has a service for use in private.

··· Significant Loss or Death ···

In the context of worship. When there is a death within the community of faith, a white carnation may be placed on the altar, and the death may be announced during the gathering. The carnation may be given to the family at the time of the funeral or memorial service. If other types of significant loss are lifted up by an individual during the gathering, they, too, become prayer concerns.

Once a year the congregation may wish to provide a time to remember those who have died during the previous year, as well as to remember all loved ones who have died. This service is also used to dedicate any memorials that were given during the year. The service of remembrance presented below is only an example of such a service.

In private. Any number of grief materials are available and are provided to the individual or family suffering the significant loss. In the case of a suicide, we give *Mourning after Suicide,* and where a child is affected by the loss, the booklet *Water Bugs and Dragonflies* is presented. If the significant loss is a divorce, then the booklet *Life after Divorce* is presented.[8]

The Celebration of Remembrance

Explanation of Purpose and Procedure

The lighting of the Christ candle commemorates members who have died during the past year.

Leader: Sustained by faith in our risen Savior, comforted by precious memories and by the Holy Spirit, we kindle the Christ candle in remembrance of *(name[s] of deceased).* As this light burns pure and clear, so may the blessed memory of our dear sister(s)/ brother(s) illumine our souls.

The candle is lit.

Congregation: His/her/their memory is precious and a blessing.

All: Amen.

In remembrance of loved ones who have died, members and friends come forward, one at a time, to light a candle at the Christ candle. They state the name of the person or persons for whom their candle is lit, and take a place around the outer walls of the sanctuary.

Silence of Remembrance

Closing Unison Prayer of Thanksgiving

All: This is a sacred moment. Our candles of love and remembrance
            burn brightly. We realize that a link has been broken in the chain
            which has bound us together, yet strong bonds of home and
            church and love continue to bind us to one another. We give
            thanks for the blessings of life, of companionship, and of
            memory. We are grateful for the strength and faith that sustained
            us in the hour of our bereavement. Though sorrow lingers, we
            have learned that love is stronger than death. Though our loved
            ones are beyond our sight, we do not despair, for we both sense
            our beloved in our hearts as a living presence, and affirm our
            faith that our beloved lives forever in Christ. All praise be to
            God, forever and ever. Amen.

All extinguish their candles and return to their seats.

Closing Hymn

Sing a hymn, usually "For All the Saints."

··· Reconciliation ···

In the context of worship. The Book of Worship, referred to above, has an
order for corporate reconciliation. Such an order may be useful in times
related to strife within a congregation or with national or international strife,
or it may be used in preparation for Holy Communion.

In private. See the home gathering celebration for dealing with "The Overwhelming Sense of Sin/Brokenness and Reconciliation" on pages 80–83.

The Act of Reconciliation and Presentation of Offerings and Gifts

This act of reconciliation may be used during Lent each year but can be used at other appropriate times as well. It follows the opening or processional hymn. The main reason for its use early in the service is to allow the children to participate both in the reconciliation and in the presentation of special gifts.

Leader: Jesus said, "So if you are about to offer your gift to God at the altar, and there you remember that your brother (or sister) has something against you, leave your gift there in front of the altar, go at once and make peace with your brother (or sister), and then come back and offer your gift to God."

The apostle Paul told us, "God was in Christ reconciling the world to God, and entrusting to us the ministry of reconciliation." Therefore, let us make peace and be reconciled to one another.

Members of the congregation face each other across the center aisle. Assign groupings for the following call for forgiveness.

Congregation 1: I stand before you as one who is broken. I ask you to forgive me, and to restore me to wholeness.

Congregation 2: I forgive you. God forgives you. Receive God's healing and wholeness.

I stand before you as one who is broken. I ask you to forgive me, and to restore me to wholeness.

Congregation 1: I forgive you. God forgives you. Receive God's healing and wholeness.

Leader: The healing, forgiving Spirit of God offers us all wholeness. Let us pass the shalom, the peace of God, to one another, in whatever way we feel comfortable. When you have done so, please be seated.

The peace is passed.

Leader: Reconciled to one another in Christ, we may now present our gifts to God. Does anyone have a special gift to present at this time?

Allow time for these gifts to be presented.

Leader: Let us present our tithes and our offerings.

Celebrating Times Related to Our Faith Journey and Church Life

··· Baptism/Dedication ···

In the context of worship. When a child is born to a family in the congregation, a rose may be placed on the altar. This rose may be pressed and presented to the family at the time of baptism or dedication. Along with an appropriate certificate, the family may be given a small, wooden cradle cross for the child. Parents and godparents or sponsors are presented with booklets describing their responsibilities. Some congregations present the family with a baptismal candle, which is then used on the anniversary of baptism.

A service of baptism is not provided in *Celebrate Life,* for most denominations provide one in their books of worship or in their hymnals. The United Church of Christ, while recognizing the validity of infant dedication and believers' baptism, does not provide one, so the following is offered.

A Rite of Dedication

The Presentation

Leader: Members of Christ's family, I present to you *(names of the family)*, together with *(child's name)*, whose coming into their home they now acknowledge with gratitude and faith and with a desire to dedicate him/her to God. "Some people brought children to Jesus for him to place his hands on them, but the disciples scolded the people."

Congregation: "When Jesus noticed this, he . . . said to his disciples, 'Let the children come to me and do not stop them, because the kingdom of God belongs to such as these.'"

Leader: "I assure you that whoever does not receive the kingdom of God like a child will never enter it."

Congregation: Then he took the children in his arms, placed his hands on each of them, and blessed them.

Leader: Within the family of Christ, the birth of a child is an occasion for thanksgiving. Life is God's gift, and children are a heritage from God. Therefore, we who are entrusted with their care are given both great responsibility and great opportunity.

Congregation: All praise be to God for so favoring us with the birth of this child.

The Prayer

All: O God, we offer the gratitude of our hearts for the gift of (*child's name*), for the joy that has come to this family and the touch of your Spirit that has led them to this time and place of dedication. Continue to pour out your Spirit upon them and upon all of us, that we may abound in your love; through Jesus Christ our Savior. Amen.

The Naming

Leader: What name do you now give your child?

Parents (*placing hands on child's head*): We name you . . .

The Thanksgiving and Dedication

Leader: In accepting (*child's name*) as a gift from God, acknowledge now your faith in Jesus Christ and the responsibility that God has placed upon you.

Parents: We receive (*child's name*) from the hand of a loving Creator. With humility and hope we dedicate her/him to God and accept the obligation which is ours to love and nurture her/him and to lead her/him to Christian faith by our teaching and example. We ask for the power of the Holy Spirit and the support of the church.

Leader (*to congregation*): The church is the family of Christ, the community in which we grow in faith and commitment. Will you take

this child into your care and offer support to these parents who
have requested it?

Congregation: We rejoice to take *(child's name)* under our care. We seek
God's grace to be a community in which the gospel is truly lived
out. We will support this family in the nurture of the Christian
faith, and in love.

Leader (*placing hands on the child's head*): *(Name of child),* may the eternal God bless and watch over you. May Jesus Christ incorporate
you into his death and resurrection through baptism when you
are ready to receive him on your own. May the Holy Spirit guide,
direct, and empower you, now and always.

All: Amen.

The Gloria Patri

Sing or say the Gloria Patri together.

··· When a Member Moves ···

When members of the church move out of the community, there should be
some significant way both to honor them and to remind them that they do
not go forth alone. They may be invited forward at the conclusion of worship
to receive a picture of the church or some other appropriate token. They may
also be presented with a traveling letter. This is a letter of introduction to a
community of faith in the new community where they will live. As they face
the congregation, the congregation could stand and sing "Shalom, My
Friends" or some other particularly meaningful song as a benediction. This
could be followed with a special coffee.

Special Sunday Celebrations

There are other ways a congregation can strengthen the bridge between home and church, and span the personal-versus-corporate faith gap spoken of earlier. For example, special Sunday celebrations can be held monthly; these are specifically designed to help in the recalling, the reliving, the re-creating, and the revisiting of the transforming moments of the faith community; they are our way of helping to transmit our faith to the next generation.

The Sunday bulletin can include pictures to help even the youngest children to a better understanding of what is taking place in worship. Families should be encouraged to sit together so that parents can better assist the children in the various aspects of worship. A congregation may even have "adopt-a-family" Sundays, where adults who do not have children in worship are invited to become an adopted parent and to sit with a family with children.

A number of items regularly used in the home gathering celebrations may be included in the regular worship and in special Sunday celebrations, including the words used in lighting the candles and in blessing the children.

Special Sunday Celebrations in a Typical Year

January—Festival of Talents Sunday

This should vary from year to year. The example we share below is in recognition of the talents of church musicians.

February—Shalom Sunday

This is a time set aside as a day of reconciliation and healing. It is a day that should focus on the shalom, the wholeness that comes from God. This is an appropriate way to lead into Lent and a good opportunity to introduce the act of reconciliation and presentation of gifts described earlier. The order for corporate reconciliation or the order for corporate healing in the UCC's *Book of Worship*, also mentioned earlier, would be appropriate to use on this day.

March—Vocations Sunday

This is a day on which our individual calling as a Christian is lifted up and honored. Each year a different major category of endeavor can be emphasized (for example, medical services, educational services, agricultural services, etc.). A sample service is included below.

April—Celebration of the Earth Sunday

This comes at different times and under different names in various communities. Rogation Sunday, the Sunday before Ascension day, has traditionally been a time of prayer for the earth and for agriculture; it often includes a ceremony of blessing the earth. For churches in rural areas, this continues to be a meaningful celebration as spring planting is usually under way.

May—Festival of the Christian Home Sunday

Every few years, we utilize this time for the renewal of vows. We include one such marriage-renewal service below.

June—Mission Sunday

The focus of this day is on the various aspects of the church's denominational mission efforts around the world. It is also a day for the congregation to focus on its own special mission projects.

July—Community-Building Sunday

The church as a special community of the body of Christ is emphasized on this Sunday. If an outdoor setting is available, this is a good opportunity for the annual picnic of the congregation, with time built in for community-building games and other activities.

August—Renewal Sunday

This is a day when our personal growth in Christ through the Holy Spirit is emphasized. There may be a display of tapes/books/CDs and the like that could be used for personal devotionals. Worship would focus on various methods of renewal, including spiritual disciplines and spiritual retreats. In fact, a whole day could be set aside for a retreat.

September—Recovenanting Sunday

This is a day designed to renew the congregation's covenantal relationship with God, with one another, and in particular with the children and staff of the church school as they begin another year of study together. Check with your denominational offices for worship materials for this Sunday.

October—Philoxenia Sunday

Philoxenia means "love of strangers." This a day when a congregation can honor the "strangers in our midst"—that is, a day when new people in the community can be welcomed even if they belong to another church. It should be made clear that it is a gesture of good will and not an attempt to proselytize or convert visitors. A Philoxenia potluck could follow the service.

November—Harvest or Thanksgiving Sunday

This is a familiar day for most congregations, and materials for its celebration can be secured from many places.

December—Celebration of Advent Sunday

In many ways, the whole period of Advent is a time of recalling, reliving, recreating, and revisiting our heritage. Emphasis is on the new church year, on the ancient hope for a messiah, on preparation to receive the Christchild. Celebration of Advent Sunday is a good time for a children's Christmas presentation.

··· Festival of Talents ···

The Recognition and Appreciation of
Our Church Musicians[9]

Leader: God is with you.

Congregation: And also with you.

Leader: O God, we thank you for music and its wondrous power to touch and heal and strengthen; under its spell the closed doors of the human spirit are unlocked, and our hearts are moved to respond to you in worship. We praise you for this most precious gift.

Observe a moment of silence.

Leader: Let everything that lives praise God.

Congregation: Thanks be to God!

Leader: We thank you for all those who, entrusted with this gift, have "composed musical tunes and set forth verses in writing." Living on among us in their works, they have enriched our lives wonderfully and exalted you in the liturgy of your church. We praise you for all writers of your songs.

Observe a moment of silence.

Leader: Let everything that lives praise God.

Congregation: Thanks be to God!

Leader: We thank you for all who teach music, interpreting the music born in the souls of others, and bringing gifts to fruition in many generations of music students. We thank you for all who play music, sharing with us their heartfelt understanding of it. We thank you for all who sing music as it wells up within them.

Observe a moment of silence.

Leader: Let everything that lives praise God.

Congregation: Thanks be to God!

Leader: And finally, we thank you for all who day by day, particularly in our congregation, enable us to sing your song in many ways, accompanying it on organ and trumpet, piano and bells, and many other instruments, leading it with the beauty of the solo voice and the harmony of combined voices, enriching it with new forms of music and old familiar ways. We praise you for the ministry of music in this church and all who are instrumental in bringing it to pass.

Observe a moment of silence.

Leader: Let everything that lives praise God.

Congregation: Thanks be to God! Amen. Amen.

The Congregation's Song of Thanksgiving for Church Musicians

This song is sung to the tune of I LOVE TO TELL THE STORY and was written by Peter Young, 1994.

> You help prepare our spirit to worship God each week,
> to offer praise and glory, God's precious truth to seek.
> You help to lift our spirits, bring joy and comfort, too.
> You share the old, old story with music fresh and new.
> We love to hear your voices, and instruments so fine.
> We thank you for your music, it always sounds divine.

··· Vocations Sunday ···

The Recognition of Our Calling to Ministry, in Particular Those Who Serve in the Field of Education

Leader: The Holy Spirit bestows on the community diverse and complementary gifts. These are for the common good of the whole people and are manifested in acts of service within the community and to the world. They may be gifts of communicating the gospel in word and deed, gifts of healing, gifts of praying, gifts of teaching and learning, gifts of serving, gifts of guiding and following, gifts of inspiration and vision. All members are called to discover, with the help of the community, the gifts they have received and to use them for the building up of the Church and for the service of the world to which the Church is sent.[10]

These words, from *Baptism, Eucharist and Ministry*, of the Faith and Order Commission of the World Council of Churches, recognize the calling of all Christians to be ministers, servants of God both in the church and in the world. These words recognize the diversity of gifts and forms of ministry described by the apostle Paul when he wrote: "Now there are varieties of gifts, but the same Spirit; and there are varieties of services, but the same Lord; and there are varieties of activities, but it is the same God who activates all of them in everyone. To each is given the manifestation of the Spirit for the common good" (1 Cor. 12:4–7).

On this day we celebrate our calling as it is carried out in our daily occupation. In particular, we honor this day those who minister in the field of education, and we commission them to this ministry in the years ahead.

Let us give thanks to God for calling us to serve in this world.

Congregation: O God, we know that you call us to serve our neighbor in love, not only in the church, but also in the world in which we live and work.

Leader: For those who minister to the needs of this world through their various occupations,

Congregation: We give you thanks, O God.

Leader: For those who minister to the needs of this world through their volunteer efforts,

Congregation: We give you thanks, O God.

Leader: For those who minister to the needs of this world through their prayers and visits,

Congregation: We give you thanks, O God.

Leader: For those whose efforts are often unseen and unsung, but who contribute significantly to Christ's ministry in the world,

Congregation: We give you thanks, O God.

Leader: For those who minister to the faith community in various capacities: teachers, leaders and officers, musicians, ushers, readers, acolytes, kitchen workers, pastors, secretaries, custodians, missionaries,

Congregation: We give you thanks, O God.

Leader: Faithful and ever-present God, we give special thanks this day for all who minister in the field of education. We pray for teachers and administrators and all others whose skills and talents aid in the ministry of education.

Congregation: May they recognize their own creativity, our thankfulness for their ministry, and our caring support.

Leader: We pray that you will send them forth with a true sense of calling as your servants in the service of humankind.

Congregation: May they use their gifts wisely and well.

Leader: We pray for students of all ages.

Congregation: May they experience the joy of learning.

Leader: We pray for all legislators, school board members, and all others who are concerned with the well-being of education—teachers and learners alike.

Congregation: May they seek your guidance and do your will.

Leader: Gracious God, grant these prayers in the name of Jesus Christ, our expert teacher, who came that we might have life abundant.

Congregation: Amen.

Certificates of appreciation are presented.

··· Festival of the Christian Home ···

The following ritual is conducted after the sermon.

The Renewal of Marriage Vows

Leader: If there is any couple here this morning who would like to renew your marriage vows and to recommit yourselves to each other in the spirit of Christ, please stand so that you can comfortably face each other. Please hold hands.

Wives, please say your husband's name and repeat after me:

Wife: I am blessed to be your wife, and I promise anew to love and sustain you in the covenant of marriage, with deep commitment, open and honest communication, abiding compassion and companionship, in sickness and in health, in plenty and in want, in joy and in sorrow, with Christ as our Sovereign, as long as we both shall live.

Leader: Husbands, please say your wife's name and repeat after me.

Husband: I am blessed to be your husband, and I promise anew to love and sustain you in the covenant of marriage, with deep commitment, open and honest communication, abiding compassion and companionship, in sickness and in health, in plenty and in want, in joy and in sorrow, with Christ as our Sovereign, as long as we both shall live.

Leader: Those whom God has joined together let no one separate. You have spoken again your covenant of love. God grant you grace to fulfill, in your life together, the solemn promises you made in the springtime of your love and which you have renewed today in the presence of God, and in the midst of your larger family in Christ.

The Song of Celebration

Sing "O Perfect Love."

Notes

Preface

1. Tom F. Driver, *The Magic of Ritual: Our Need for Liberating Rites That Transform Our Lives and Our Communities* (San Francisco: Harper, 1991), 32.
2. Robert N. Bellah et al., *Habits of the Heart* (New York: Harper & Row, 1985).
3. James P. Shaughnessy, ed., *Roots of Ritual* (Grand Rapids, Mich.: William B. Eerdmans, 1973), 99.

Introduction: Saying Yes to Life

1. Sister Corita (Kent), *Footnotes and Headlines* (Philadelphia: United Church Press, 1967), 2.
2. Arnold van Gennep, *The Rites of Passage,* trans. Monika B. Vizedom and Gabrielle L. Chaffee (Chicago: University of Chicago Press, 1960).
3. James Russell Lowell, "Once to Every Man and Nation," in *The Pilgrim Hymnal* (New York: The Pilgrim Press, 1931), 441.
4. Sister Corita, *Footnotes and Headlines.*
5. Driver, *Magic of Ritual,* 7.
6. Central Conference of American Rabbis, *A Shabbat Manual* (New York: KTAV Publishing House, 1972), 1.
7. Driver, *Magic of Ritual,* 44.
8. Sarah Wenger Shenk, *Why Not Celebrate!* (Intercourse, Pa.: Good Books, 1987), 7–8.
9. Central Conference of American Rabbis, *Shabbat Manual,* 1.
10. Bellah et al., *Habits of the Heart,* vii.
11. Ibid., 142.
12. Loren B. Mead, *The Once and Future Church* (Washington, D.C.: Alban Institute, 1991), 8.
13. Ibid.
14. Ibid.

Celebratory Rituals for the Home

1. James D. G. Dunn, "Jesus, Table-Fellowship, and Qumran," in *Jesus and the Dead Sea Scrolls,* ed. James H. Charlesworth (New York: Doubleday, 1993), 254; A. J. Jeremias, *New Testament Theology, Vol. 1: The Proclamation of Jesus* (London: 1971), 115.

2. John Patton, "Caring for Our Generations," *The Christian Century,* March 2, 1988, 211.

3. Craig Douglas Erickson, *Participating in Worship: History, Theory, and Practice* (Louisville, Ky.: Westminster/John Knox Press, 1989), 143–44.

4. Jack W. Lundin, *Celebrations for Special Days and Occasions* (New York: Harper & Row, 1971), 3–5.

5. *The New Century Hymnal* (Cleveland: The Pilgrim Press, 1995).

6. Driver, *Magic of Ritual,* 213–16.

7. This blessing is based on Numbers 6:24–26. It is used in many home gathering rituals.

8. Lundin, *Celebrations for Special Days,* 71–72.

9. Dorothy Payne, *Life after Divorce* (New York: The Pilgrim Press, 1982), 4, 23.

10. George W. Cooke, "Down in My Heart."

11. *The United Church of Christ Book of Worship* (New York: United Church of Christ Office for Church Life and Leadership, 1986).

12. Original words by Daniel Iverson. Adaptation by Peter Young, 1994.

13. Christine E. Gudorf, "The Worst Sexual Sin: Sexual Violence and the Church," *The Christian Century,* January 6–13, 1993.

14. Lois A. Bloom, *Mourning after Suicide* (New York: The Pilgrim Press, 1987), 24.

15. Hoyt L. Hickman, Don E. Saliers, Laurence H. Stookey, and James F. White, *The Handbook of the Christian Year* (Nashville, Tenn.: Abingdon Press, 1988), 219.

Celebratory Rituals for the Church

1. Robert L. Browning and Roy A. Reed, *The Sacraments in Religious Education and Liturgy* (Birmingham, Ala.: Religious Education Press, 1985), 21.

2. Ibid., 220.

3. John Shelby Spong, *Resurrection: Myth or Reality* (San Francisco: HarperCollins, 1944), 33.

4. Marva J. Dawn, *Reaching Out without Dumbing Down* (Grand Rapids, Mich.: William B. Eerdmans, 1995), 4.

5. Clarissa Pinkola Estés, *Women Who Run with the Wolves* (New York: Ballantine Books, 1992), 197.

6. From *The United Church of Christ Book of Worship,* 431–38ff.

7. John E. Biegert, *Looking Up . . . While Lying Down* (Cleveland: The Pilgrim Press, 1978), and Geneva M. Butz et al., *Color Me Well* (Cleveland: The Pilgrim Press, 1986).

8. Bloom, *Mourning after Suicide;* Doris Stickney, *Water Bugs and Dragonflies* (Cleveland: The Pilgrim Press, 1997); and Payne, *Life after Divorce.*

9. "A Thanksgiving for Music and Musicians," adapted from *The Wideness of God's Mercy,* vol. 1, by Jeffery W. Rowthorn.

10. *Baptism, Eucharist and Ministry* (Geneva: World Council of Churches, 1982), 20.

Additional Resources

Rituals

Browning, Robert L., and Roy A. Reed. *The Sacraments in Religious Education and Liturgy.* Birmingham, Ala.: Religious Education Press, 1985.

De Jesús, José Abraham. *The Liturgy of Learning: An Approach to Whole Church Education.* Cleveland: United Church Board for Homeland Ministries, 1996.

Driver, Tom F. *The Magic of Ritual: Our Need for Liberating Rites That Transform Our Lives and Our Communities.* San Francisco: Harper, 1991.

Fried, Martha Nemes, and Morton H. Fried. *Transitions: Four Rituals in Eight Cultures.* New York: Penguin Books, 1980.

Jones, Cheslyn, Geoffrey Wainwright, and Edward Yarnold, eds. *The Study of Liturgy.* New York: Oxford University Press, 1978.

Mahdi, Louise Carus, Steven Foster, and Meredith Little, eds. *Betwixt and Between: Patterns of Masculine and Feminine Initiation.* La Salle, Ill.: Open Court, 1993.

Neville, Gwen Kennedy, and John H. Westerhoff III. *Learning through Liturgy.* New York: Seabury Press, 1978.

Ramshaw, Elaine. *Ritual and Pastoral Care.* Philadelphia: Fortress Press, 1987.

Westerhoff, John H., III. *A Pilgrim People: Learning through the Church Year.* Minneapolis: Winston Press, 1984.

Westerhoff, John H., III, and William H. Willimon. *Liturgy and Learning through the Life Cycle.* Minneapolis: Winston Press, 1980.

Home Rituals

Cardozo, Arlene Rossen. *Jewish Family Celebrations: The Sabbath, Festivals, and Ceremonies.* New York: St. Martin's Press, 1982.

Castle, Tony. *Celebrations for the Family.* Ann Arbor, Mich.: Servant Books, 1986.

Cronin, Gaynell. *Sunday throughout the Week.* Notre Dame, Ind.: Ave Maria Press, 1981.

Daily Prayer: The Worship of God. Supplemental Liturgical Resource No. 5. Philadelphia: Westminster Press, 1987.

Gaither, Gloria, and Shirley Dobson. *Let's Make a Memory.* Waco, Tex.: Word Books, 1983.

Hopkins, Mary. *Celebrating Family Prayer Services.* New York: Paulist Press, 1975.

Huck, Gabe. *A Book of Family Prayer.* New York: Seabury Press, 1983.

Ingram, Kristen Johnson. *Family Worship through the Year: Ideas for Every Season, Special Days, and Holidays.* Valley Forge, Pa.: Judson Press, 1984.

Lamb, Sister Jane Marie, ed. *Bittersweet . . . Hellogoodbye.* Belleville, Ill.: Charis Communications, 1988. A resource for planning a farewell ritual when a baby dies.

Lundin, Jack W. *Celebrations for Special Days and Occasions.* New York: Harper & Row, 1971.

Maslin, Simeon J., ed. *Gates of Mitzvah: A Guide to the Jewish Life Cycle.* New York: Central Conference of American Rabbis, 1979.

Nelson, Gertrud Mueller. *To Dance with God: Family Ritual and Community Celebration.* Mahwah, N.J.: Paulist Press, 1986. A focus on the church year.

Shenk, Sara Wenger. *Why Not Celebrate!* Intercourse, Pa.: Good Books, 1987.

Sorlien, Sandra. *Keeping Christmas, Activities and Devotions for the Twelve Days of Christmas.* Minneapolis: Augsburg, 1982.

Stern, Chaim, ed. *Gates of the House: The New Union Home Prayerbook.* New York: Central Conference of American Rabbis, 1977.

Warfield-Coppock, Nsenga, and Aminifu R. Harvey. *A Rites of Passage Resource Manual.* New York: United Church of Christ Commission for Racial Justice, 1989. Teenage pregnancy prevention; traditional African rites of passage.

Washington, Donna L. *The Story of Kwanzaa.* New York: HarperCollins, 1996.

Webb, Barbara Owen. *Devotions for Families: Building Blocks of Christian Life.* Valley Forge, Pa.: Judson Press, 1976.

Zimmerman, Martha. *Celebrate the Feasts of the Old Testament in Your Own Home or Church.* Minneapolis: Bethany House, 1981.

Church Rituals

Blessings and Consecrations: A Book of Occasional Services. Supplemental Worship Resources No. 14. Nashville, Tenn.: Abingdon Press, 1984.

Davidson, Robert G., ed. *Creative Ideas for Advent.* Prescott, Ariz.: Educational Ministries, 1980.

————. *Creative Ideas for Lent.* Prescott, Ariz.: Educational Ministries, 1985.

Duck, Ruth C., ed. Bread for the Journey. New York: The Pilgrim Press, 1982. Resources for worship.

————. *Flames of the Spirit.* New York: Pilgrim Press, 1985. Resources for worship.

Duck, Ruth C., and Maren C. Tirabassi, eds. *Touch Holiness.* New York: The Pilgrim Press, 1990. Resources for worship.

Hickman, Hoyt L., Don E. Saliers, Laurence Hull Stookey, and James F. White. *The New Handbook of the Christian Year.* Nashville, Tenn.: Abingdon Press, 1992.

Lee, Bernard J., ed. *Alternative Futures for Worship.* Collegeville, Minn.: Liturgical Press, 1987. A seven-volume look at the future of liturgy: 1. General Introduction; 2. Baptism and Confirmation; 3. The Eucharist; 4. Reconciliation; 5. Christian Marriage; 6. Leadership Ministry in Community; and 7. Anointing of the Sick.

McMane, Martie. *Worship Comes Alive.* Cleveland: United Church Board for Homeland Ministries, 1991. A resource book for music and the arts.

Rowthorn, Jeffrey W. *The Wideness of God's Mercy: Litanies to Enlarge Our Prayer.* Minneapolis: Winston Press, 1985. Two volumes: 1. Prayers for the Church; 2. Prayers for the World.

Watkins, Keith, ed. *Thankful Praise: A Resource for Christian Worship.* St. Louis: CBP Press, 1987.